THE FASHION ICONS

G U C C I

Alison James

First Published Danann Media Publishing Limited 2024

CAT NO: SON0591

Photography courtesy of

Getty images:

Scott Gries
PATRICK HERTZOG/AFP
J.P. MOCZULSKI/AFP
Kevin Mazur Archive/WireImage
Michael Ochs Archives
Don Arnold/WireImage
Giuseppe Aresu/Bloomberg
Terry Fincher
KMazur/WireImage
Ron Galella Collection
Venturelli/WireImage
Laurent MAOUS/Gamma-Rapho
Jeff Kravitz/FilmMagic, Inc
Vittorio Zunino Celotto
Victor VIRGILE/Gamma-Rapho
Antonio de Moraes Barros Filho/WireImage
Roberto Carnevali
Karwai Tang/WireImage
Sonia Moskowitz
Patrick McMullan
Dia Dipasupil/FilmMagic
Touring Club Italiano
Daniele Venturelli
Victor VIRGILE/Gamma-Rapho
Davide Maestri/WWD/Penske Media
Giovanni Giannoni/WWD/Penske Media
Delphine Achard/WWD/Penske Media
Mauricio Miranda/WWD/Penske Media
David Yoder/WWD/Penske Media
Fairchild Archive/Penske Media
Benjamin Girette/Bloomber
GABRIEL BOUYS/AFP
Art Streiber/Penske Media
ANACLETO RAPPING

Alamy:

Retro AdArchives
Everett Collection Inc
Stephen Lloyd Hong Kong SAR
Cineclassico
Cavan Images
Rod Olukoya
dpa picture alliance
Mark Green
Associated Press
Chronicle
Directphoto Collection
TCD/Prod.DB
Sipa US
Abaca Press
Kristina Blokhin

Other images, Wiki Commons

Book design Darren Grice at Ctrl-d
Proof reader Juliette O'Neil

Made in EU.
ISBN: 978-1-915343-47-5

CONTENTS

INTRODUCTION

When Guccio Gucci started his small luggage company in Florence in 1921, he can never have dreamed it would evolve into the iconic, global billion-dollar brand it is today. The House - synonymous with classic design, elegance, luxury and quality - boasts an instantly recognisable signature style all of its own. The double G logo; the bar-and-horsebit belt, shoe and bag accessory; the bamboo-handle handbag; the loafer, the Flora design. . . all have enabled Gucci to penetrate mainstream culture like no other Italian label in history.

The company's initial expansion took place while Guccio's eldest son, Aldo, was at the helm. A flamboyant businessman, he transformed the business into the place for the emerging jet-set to shop for accessories. By the end of the 1960s everyone from Queen Elizabeth II to Elizabeth Taylor was a customer and by the early '70s, the lean silhouettes, fur-lined coats, and satin lapels which would become the Gucci classics of that era began to appear. However, as the 1980s dawned, over licensing had tarnished the label's high-end identity, and the sons and grandsons of Guccio were at war. In 1993 the family lost control of the, by then, near-bankrupt company which floundered until a few years into the tenure of a young Texan designer named Tom Ford who became Creative Director in 1994. Ford's 'sexy, sensual, f**k-me clothes' were immediately adopted by 'A' listers, making Gucci a success again – both financially and creatively. From 2005 till 2015, former Gucci accessories designer Frida Giannini held the reins at this formerly equestrian-themed business but when profits fell and her designs failed to light a sartorial spark, her assistant Alessandro Michele replaced her. For eight years Michele, with his whimsical, gender-fluid, highly romantic and uber-original vision, hardly put a horse-bit loafer wrong, but nothing lasts forever – especially in the high-octane world of high-end fashion – and at the end of 2022, Michele's tenure came to a sudden end.

As Gucci enters yet another new era under the direction and leadership of Sabato De Sarno, we take a look back at the brand, chart its evolution and wonder at its creations, designs and sartorial genius. From its relatively humble beginnings as a manufacturer of luggage, through good times and bad – including vicious family in-fights, scandal and even murder - to becoming the influential, innovative haute-couture, global power house it is today.

EARLY DAYS

'He was a man of great taste which we all inherited. His imprint was on every item he sold'

Aldo Gucci on his father Guccio, founder of the House of Gucci

If the straw hat and leather goods business owned by the parents of House of Gucci founder Guccio Giovanbattista Giacinto Dario Maria had been successful, it's quite possible that the iconic fashion brand never would have existed. Guccio, born in Florence in March 1881 to Gabriello Gucci and his wife Elena Santini, fled to London in 1897, following his father's bankruptcy and the collapse of the family business. Once he had arrived in what was then the greatest city in the world, Guccio, aged just 16, found work at the uber-luxurious and prestigious Savoy Hotel on the Strand. The Savoy was, at that time, at the very zenith of technology – it being the first hotel in the world to install electric lighting, prototype telephones and an electric lift or elevator. During his time there, Guccio was employed firstly as a dish washer before moving on to becoming a waiter, bellhop and concierge.

It was while he was working as an elevator attendant that he noticed the beautifully-crafted, leather suitcases and trunks that the elite guests of the hotel travelled with. An alert, intelligent and ambitious youth, Guccio observed these wealthy folk, taking in their fashionable style, clothing, accessories, jewellery, manners, habits – and, most importantly, their luxurious luggage. He became fascinated by London's craftsmen and the manufacturers of leather goods, in particular H.J Cave and Sons, the most prestigious – and expensive – maker of luggage in Great Britain. Inspired by what he saw, Guccio was determined that at some point in the not-too-

ABOVE: Guccio gucci
RIGHT: Exterior and restaurant of Savoy, circa 1900

MAX
COWPER

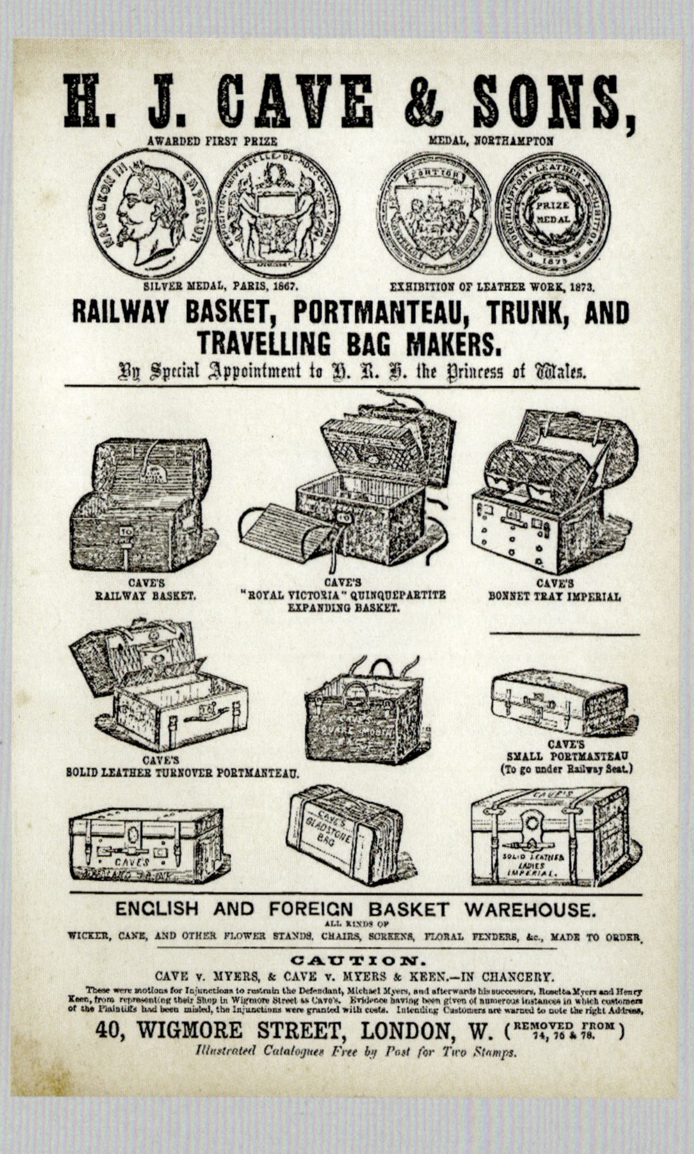

distant future he would succeed where his father had failed and set up his own high-quality leather-goods company.

'One day,' he is believed to have said, *'luggage like this will bear my name.'*

With a new vision of what he wanted his life's work to be, Guccio returned to Florence in 1902, where after a short spell working in the antiques trade, he trained and then worked as a leather goods craftsman for Valigeria Franzi, a prestigious luggage company favoured by the wealthy, including royalty and nobility. It was at Franzi that Guccio learned craftsmanship and fine-tuned his talent as a creator of outstanding pieces of luggage, honing his craft there for well over 15 years. As time went on, he began to design and produce leather goods, inspiring him to fulfil his long-held ambition of opening his own business. Guccio, had by this time, been married for almost 20 years to his seamstress wife Alda Calvelli. The couple had a daughter and three sons – a fourth having died in childhood. Guccio also adopted Alda's son from a previous relationship. On a Sunday afternoon stroll around Florence with Aida in early 1921, Guccio noticed a small shop for rent on the Via della Vigna Nuova, a side street in between the elegant thoroughfares of the Via Tornabuoni and Piazza Goldoni on the banks of the river Arno. Could this be it? Would it be possible for him to finally open his own store in the space? Having discussed the possibility with his wife, Guccio decided it was. Using his savings and a loan from an acquaintance, he founded La Casa Gucci (House of Gucci) and opened his first shop. From these decidedly humble beginnings, what would become an international, multi-billion powerhouse of a fashion brand was officially founded. At the time, of course, no one could have predicted just how mighty La Casa Gucci would one day become.

The store's first customers were mainly horsemen

ABOVE: Advert for H.J. Cave and Sons

seeking out leather accessories - horse sports at that time were considered elite and the city's wealthy equestrians quickly recognised the quality of Gucci products. Guccio was keen to expand his customer base. He aspired to a certain elegance and style himself, and was always impeccably turned out in fine shirts and crisply pressed suits. With the classic designs of his goods displaying both inspiration from London and the skilled craftsmanship of local Tuscan artisans, Gucci's luxurious leather suitcases, bags, trunks and equestrian items were in a class of their own. Guccio hoped to attract an exclusive clientele with imported German and English luggage in addition to his own, 'home-grown' pieces. Targeting the Florentine rich, the high bourgeoisie and the nobility, his reputation grew. As the business expanded, Guccio was able to extend the small workshop at the back of his store and hire a more skilful group of artisans to work on the custom-made goods. These men were more like artists than manufacturing workers, and produced high-quality bags made from delicate kidskin and chamois leather - also telescope purses and suitcases inspired by the Gladstone bags Guccio had seen in London while working at the Savoy. Other lines included car robe carriers, shoe boxes and bed linen carriers – in those days the upper class always travelled with their own bed linen when holidaying. Although Guccio organized his workrooms, now housing 60 leather workers, for industrial methods of production, he maintained traditional aspects of fabrication. Gucci employed workers skilled in basic Florentine leather craft who were especially attentive to the art of finishing. With expansion, he was able to introduce machine stitching.

Despite a near brush with bankruptcy in the mid 1920s, when the combination of suppliers who had given Guccio credit when first setting up the business demanded payment and customers failing to pay their bills almost led to the business going under, ultimately the brand thrived – so much so that a second Gucci store was opened in Florence on the Via del Parione before the 1920s were out. The Gucci range of travelling leather bags were of the highest quality with Anglophile Guccio continuing to be inspired by classic British design and manufacturing. As the 1930s dawned, La Casa Gucci was the place to purchase leather and equestrian goods with many well-heeled customers travelling from overseas to buy. By this time, Guccio and his team had expanded their range beyond luggage to include gloves, shoes, belts and ladies' bags. He was something of a visionary with regards to handbags for women, recognising that the female half of the population were becoming increasingly emancipated as the 1930s progressed. He launched his first specifically marketed women's handbag in 1937. While the equestrian side of his business had, by this time, started to fall away, Guccio never lost his liking for equestrian style. This was reflected in his designs. Indeed, it was to become the trade-mark, the signature, the very calling card of La Casa Gucci. . .

FATHER, SONS AND STATEMENT PIECES

'Aldo was a formidable character. Without his vision, Gucci would almost certainly have remained a single-store entity in the back streets of Florence'

Patricia Gucci, Aldo's daughter

From the get go, La Casa Gucci was a family business. Aida Gucci with her background as a seamstress was a great help to her husband during the early years while daughter Grimalda, sons Aldo, Vasco and Rodolfo, and step son Ugo helped out in the shops from a relatively early age. However, it was Aldo, born in 1905 and the eldest of Guccio's biological sons, who showed the most interest. Aged 16, he began working part-time at his father's first shop on Florence's Via della Vigna Nuova where his tasks included delivering packages by horse and cart to customers, sweeping the shop floor and generally tidying up. He became a full-time employee four years later once he'd gained a degree in economics at the prestigious San Marco college in Florence. Committing himself full-time to the business, he was soon to prove himself as a persuasive salesman, talented designer, savvy businessman and genius at marketing. As the 1920s gave way to the '30s, he became his father's right-hand man.

Events occurring beyond the leather goods world brought fresh challenges to the business. Following the invasion of Ethiopia in 1935 by Italy's fascist leader Benito 'Il Duce' Mussolini, the League of Nations imposed sanctions which seriously hampered the import of leather to the nation with a total of 52 countries refusing to trade with Italy. This forced Guccio, who was petrified history was repeating itself and that his business would fold as his father's had, to think outside the box. While sourcing as much leather as he could from Italian tanneries, Guccio began to experiment with other materials for his bags - introducing raffia, wood, linen and jute into the manufacturing process to lessen the leather content. Most significantly, he introduced a specially woven hemp, known as 'canapa' into the process. This fabric was hardwearing yet lightweight and soon became a Gucci trademark, especially once the firm's first signature print had been developed. The print was a pattern of small, connecting, dark brown diamond shapes printed across a tan background. It was known as the Diamante pattern and was to become the first official emblem of La Casa Gucci.

Aldo, meanwhile, was travelling around Italy and other European nations, researching into the possibility of expanding the Gucci brand to more Italian cities and also overseas – even though Guccio seemed dead set against this idea, preferring to keep things close to home. However, Aldo's persistence finally paid off and in September 1938, the first Gucci store opened in Rome on the chic Via Condotti in a historic building known as Palazzo Negri. The first two floors of this grandiose building swiftly became Gucci territory, boasting glass doors and ivory handles carved in the shape of a pile of olives – an exact copy of the door handles at the Via della Vigna Nuova shop in Florence. Inside, the store was unmistakably stylish with large glass cabinets displaying Gucci products in all their glory.

When World War Two broke out in September 1939, Guccio helped support the Italian infantry by giving part of the factory over to manufacturing boots. His canvas bags were also popular with the militia.

During the war, Guccio's other two biological sons, Vasco and Rodolfo, formerly joined the family firm. Vasco, after a short spell in the military, oversaw the factory in Florence and the wartime production of footwear. As for Rodolfo, his erstwhile career as a film star having stalled, he asked his father if he could become involved with the business. Guccio, who had never been happy about his younger son abandoning La Casa Gucci for the frivolous film world and changing his birth name for the starry sounding 'Maurizio D'Ancora', was unsure. However, he was ultimately persuaded to allow the prodigal son to return to the family fold by Aldo. The way forward-thinking Aldo saw it, once business picked up again after the war, they would need another safe pair of hands. And what was safer than family?

It was during the immediate post-war years that Gucci produced several of their classic signature pieces. The bamboo-handled bag, originally known by its code number '0633', is thought to have first seen the light of day in 1947 – the exact date is unknown. Bamboo was introduced as a material due to the ban on leather imports to Italy. The bag's creation is largely attributed to Aldo and is thought to be based on a design, incidentally with a leather handle, that he saw in London. Scrambling around to find materials to substitute for a leather handle towards the end of World War Two, Gucci's craftsmen discovered that they could use Japanese bamboo to fashion handles treated with a unique (and patented) method. These varnished bamboo handles - shaped by hand over fire, giving them their distinctive, never-seen-before look - became synonymous with Gucci while the main body of the bag was based on the shape of a saddle.

Nineteen forty-nine saw Aldo discovering and then incorporating pigskin hides into the Gucci stable. Aldo had spotted a display of skins at a trade fair in London and although taken by the natural ginger hue of the product, requested that the tanner, a Scotsman by the name of Mr Holden, have some of the skins dyed vibrant colours such as blue and green. Holden thought this a strange request but agreed to do so.

'He presented me with six skins in different colours,' Aldo was to recall. *'He shook his head saying, "It's up to you but we think they're awful!".*

Aldo, however, did not and had the skins made into bags, thus creating yet another iconic Gucci fashion item.

In 1953 Aldo created the signature 'Horsebit' loafer, incorporating into the shoe design a metallic snaffle bit, referencing a horse's mouth-bit and thus giving a nod to Gucci's equestrian heritage. Although Guccio had produced fine leather shoes with metal snaffles in the 1930s, Aldo redesigned and refined the idea. This same year, the multi-talented Aldo created a new spin on the Diamante fabric print by dreaming up the 'Double G' logo - inspired by his father's initials – and adding this to the diamond shapes. This would become one of the world's most famous and instantly recognisable logos, ultimately giving the brand world-wide recognition and adding to its success. The Gucci crest of a knight on a shield surrounded by ribbon inscribed with the family name was also added to the fabric design in some instances while charm-like reproductions of the crest itself were attached to items of luggage.

Gucci's signature branded green-red-green stripe twill trim was yet another Gucci classic born during the early 1950s – and yet another Aldo creation. As with the 'Horsebit' loafer, the stripe was inspired by the equestrian world, resembling the Italian-style girth encircling a horse's body to hold the saddle on the animal's back. The colours were chosen to represent British red and green hunting colours, thus bringing to mind further aristocratic associations such as military medals and public-school scarves. The stripes were incorporated on handbags, belts, wallets, shoes and many other products and remains an iconic Gucci logo to this day.

It was around this time that Aldo began perpetuating the myth that the Guccis were descended from noble saddle-makers to the medieval courts. In truth, they were not, as Grimalda Gucci revealed in 1987, citing that she wanted the truth to come out. What was true, however, was the first Gucci tagline launched around this time - *'Quality is remembered long after price is forgotten.'*

Having served his apprenticeship in the Florence stores, Rodolfo opened the first Gucci store in Milan in 1951 on the Via Montenapoleone, said to be the most elite thoroughfare in the city. Later that year Guccio and his three sons were invited to New York to show their collections at a small gathering for European and US buyers. Father stayed home while 'the boys' crossed the pond. Fashionistas and journalists raved about the brand, loving the quality and style of the Gucci range.

As a result, the ever-ambitious Aldo pressed to open a store in New York. Gucci Snr did not agree, saying he was old-fashioned enough to believe that the best vegetables came from his own garden! He insisted that Aldo raise the finances for the store courtesy of the bank – which Aldo promptly did. Once the money was in place, a small shop was sourced on the Savoy Plaza Hotel East Fifty-Eighth Street, just off Fifth Avenue. With help from a lawyer, Aldo incorporated the first Gucci company in the US with an initial investment of $6000. Although reportedly furious when he received news from his eldest son that he was now honorary president of the US company, Guccio, once he'd been persuaded to fly over and see the new store, started claiming that the idea had been his all along!

'You are a man of great vision,' his sycophantic friends would tell him.

Unfortunately, he was not around long enough to see how 'his vision' played out. Two weeks after the inauguration of the New York store, Guccio dropped dead of a heart attack. He was 72-years-old. His doctor later informed the family that his heart had just stopped – *'like an old watch'*. Guccio's sudden death opened up chasms within the family. He left the business divided equally between his three biological sons. His only daughter Grimalda was excluded, despite the years she had spent working for the family business where she was mostly responsible for 'maning' the cash desk at the Gucci store in Florence. It was also Grimalda's husband Giovanni Vitali who had saved La Casa Gucci from bankruptcy in 1924. According to one of Aldo's sons, Roberto, his father told him that Guccio had decreed that no woman was ever permitted to be a partner in Gucci. Grimalda received some land, a farmhouse and a modest amount of cash as her inheritance. She was fond of her brothers and asked them to include her in the running of the business but they refused. As a result, she took the case to court but lost. Not surprisingly, she was very bitter.

'What I really wanted was a part in the development of the company I'd seen grown from nothing,' she was reported as saying.

Meanwhile the trinity of Guccio's biological sons, Aldo in particular, were determined to keep their father's dream of an elite brand alive while also moving ahead with the times. They mourned their father but were also aware that his death would liberate how they ran the company. It was decided that La Casa Gucci would be divided into three areas of responsibility. Aldo was at its head in all but name and pursued his ambition of expanding the business overseas and therefore travelled much of the time. Vasco ran the factory in Florence while Rodolfo was happy in Milan. The two younger brothers were mostly happy with Aldo calling the shots as over the next few years, the Gucci brand became a global powerhouse with some of the world's biggest stars becoming the fashion house's biggest fans and supporters.

LA DOLCE VITA

'Quality is remembered long after price is forgotten'

Aldo Gucci

Movie stars, Royalty, Fashionistas, FLOTUS and POTUS. . . all manner of the great, the good and the glitterati flocked to Gucci between the mid 1950s and early '70s – widely regarded as La Casa Gucci's Golden Age. Throughout these halcyon years, the brand was driven by unprecedented creative impulse and output. The first fashion item to be feted by the film world was a wooden-handled Gucci purse clutched by Oscar winning actress Ingrid Bergman in Roberto Rossellini's film 'Stromboli'. She co-starred with a Gucci leather bag in 'Europa 51' two years later, and went on to premiere the iconic bamboo-handled bag in the 1954 movie 'Viaggio in Italia' where she also clutched a matching bamboo-handled umbrella amidst the ruins of Pompei's Grande Palaestra. So fond was the Swedish star of her Italian handbag, she was photographed carrying one while out with her children in Naples. The Gucci Bamboo also appeared in the 1955 Michelangelo Antonioni film 'Le Amiche' on the arm of Eleonora Rossi. Eleven years later it was toted by the mini-skirt-wearing actress Vanessa Redgrave in the 1960s thriller 'Blow Up'.

As the 1960s dawned, within a few years another Gucci handbag would reach iconic status due to its connection with one of the most famous women in the world. 'The Constance' – a half-moon-shaped purse with hobo-style silhouette and piston-shaped closure – had been launched in 1958. It was a departure from many of the more austere, structured bags of the era, signalling an effortless elegance

ABOVE: Gucci black leather bag with bamboo handle, 1947
RIGHT: Ingrid Bergman in Viaggio In Italia, with Gucci bag and umbrella, 1954

ABOVE: Original film posters, featuring Gucci products
RIGHT: Jackie Kennedy and 'Jackie' bag

and more contemporary feel complete with shoulder strap. While the stylish accessory had the potential to reach cult status like its sister bag 'The Bamboo', it failed to do so until it caught the eye of a certain former FLOTUS. The story goes that in 1964, five years after the Constance was first released, Jackie Kennedy Onassis wandered into a Gucci boutique and left with six of the crescent-shaped bags. From then on, she was rarely photographed without one tucked under her arm, popularising the style and prompting the house to change the name of the bag to 'the Jackie'. Its appeal was across the board with even the likes of Irish playwright and novelist Samuel Beckett owning one. He was photographed looking extremely chic with a 'Jackie' on his arm on the streets of Genoa, Italy, in 1971.

Gucci had star quality with a capital 'S'! Elizabeth Taylor, Audrey Hepburn and Sophia Loren were devotees while Queen Elizabeth II was thought to own a set of Gucci luggage. Male stars were just as smitten and lapped up the brand's men's range which included shoes, belts, jewellery, driving slippers and a man bag. Frank Sinatra is said to have owned 40-plus pairs of Gucci shoes, including the famous 'Horsebit' loafers; comedy legend Red Skelton had a set of maroon Gucci suitcases; British actor and comedian Peter Sellars owned a crocodile-skin attache case while fellow British thespian Laurence Harvey commissioned a 'bar briefcase' complete with inserts to hold ice bucket, bottles & glasses. Other famous male customers during this Gucci golden era included actors George Hamilton, James Garner, Yul Brynner, Tony Curtis, Steve McQueen and Gregory Peck. Little wonder then that shortly before his assassination in November 1963, President John F Kennedy declared that Aldo Gucci should be known as *'the first Italian ambassador of fashion'.*

TOP: Elizabeth Taylor, Audrey Hepburn & Sophia Loren
ABOVE: Vintage 'Horsebit' loafers
RIGHT: 1960s Vintage Gucci luggage advert

NOT COUNTING THE COST

Smooth travellers in the luxury class. Quintet of cases, ready to take flight in royal blue canvas, brilliantly strapped in scarlet leather, shiningly buckled in gilt. Three perfectly matched cases, stepped up in size. Impeccable hat box; light, flexible holdall, side-locking. The set costs £114 18s. or the pieces can be bought separately. All by Gucci, New Bond St, London

Pearls: Jewelcraft. Photograph by Frank Whitchurch

The Golden Girl of this Golden Age, however, the ultimate Gucci goddess, would have to be Princess Grace of Monaco, the former Hollywood film star, Grace Kelly. In 1966, 10 years after her marriage to Prince Rainier, Princess Grace visited Gucci's flagship store in Milan. While shopping, she selected one of the signature Gucci Bamboo bags. Uber-charming Rodolfo Gucci wished to present the Serene Highness with a gift – a Gucci creation - to go alongside the purchase. Princess Grace refused the offer at first but when pressed, suggested a scarf. She didn't know at the time that the brand

ABOVE: An example of a 'Flora' scarf
RIGHT: Vittorio Accornero de Testa & Grace Kelly

had made few scarves, apart from a small number measuring just 70 square centimetres cut from a very masculine stirrup-and-train-themed silk fabric. Hardly fitting for a princess. Rodolfo asked her what she had in mind. *'A floral design, perhaps?'* she replied. Ever the smooth operator, Rodolfo lied and told her that the very same design just happened to be in the work room in the last stage of production. The moment Princess Grace left the boutique on Via Montenapoleone, Rodolfo contacted Italian painter, illustrator and set designer Vittorio Accornero de Testa whom he knew from his old movie star days and asked him to design a scarf that would reflect the Princess' love of florals while also embracing her innate sense of beauty and style. De Testa came up with an explosion of flowers, a veritable floral cornucopia. Thus, the legendary 'Flora' scarf was born.

Inspired by Botticelli's 'Allegory of Spring', which depicts the nymph Chloris reborn as Flora (Spring) in a gown imprinted with poppies, roses, violets, daisies and chrysanthemums, 'Flora' was a delicate and enchanting botanical-floral composition with the addition of berries and insects – including butterflies, dragonflies, bees, butterflies, beetles and grasshoppers. The design was depicted with the care and expertise of a naturalist, and consisted of 37 vibrant colours displayed on a white background The nine floral bouquets featured were composed of lilies, ivy, poppies, cornflowers, daffodils, ranunculus, anemones, tulips and irises. The design was hand-painted onto a 90cm square of silk and delivered to Her Serene Highness as soon as it was finished. She is said to have been delighted with the gift. As was the House of Gucci. The 'Flora' became the inspiration upon which countless Gucci dresses, handbags, and even perfume would be created, with the design continuing to spawn numerous interpretations as Gucci changed creative directors over the course of the next five decades. De Testa, meanwhile, went on to design and produce a number of hand-painted scarves for Gucci over the next 15 years but none were ever as iconic as the 'Flora'.

ABOVE: Botticelli's 'Allegory of Spring'
RIGHT: Peter Sellers walking out of the 'Gucci' boutique with his children Michael and Sarah. Rome, 1966

In addition to the creation of the royal scarf, the 1960s saw the modification of the famous 'horsebit' loafers. The women's shoe became dressier with a stacked leather heel and narrow gold chain embedded into it, with matching chain displayed across the front vamp. Re-named 'Model 350', the shoe became available in seven leathers, including lizard, ostrich, alligator, reversed calf and pig skin, and also a new range of colours including pinky beige and pale almond green. By 1969, 84,000 pairs a year were being sold – 24,000 in New York City alone. At $32 a pair, the loafers were an affordable status symbol yet still beloved by the 'A' list, including Brigitte Bardot and Jane Birkin who were both pictured wearing the classic footwear. The loafers – both male and female versions – were largely responsible for making Gucci the high-powered, global fashion brand it became.

This Gucci golden age saw the expansion of Gucci stores across the world. During the 1960s and early 70s, a total of 10 new stores opened in Europe & US. A second New York shop opened in 1960, followed by outlets in London, Palm Beach and Paris. In October 1968, chez Gucci opened in Los Angeles where Aldo identified the then sleepy Rodeo Drive as a prime location for a high-end shopping thoroughfare long before it became fashionable. The open, plant-filled loggia of the store provided husbands and boyfriends with a relaxing, stylish place to sit while their womenfolk shopped. This opening was a star-studded affair, as befitted a location that was the epicentre of the movie world, and culminated in a fashion show and reception. It was on this occasion that Gucci launched their first dresses, including a long-sleeved A line gown in a silk floral print, comprising 31 colours. Three gold chains attached with mother-of-pearl buttons highlighted the Cossack-style neck and front slit on the dress while solid colours banded the neck-line, sleeves and hem-line. The following year, Gucci's first scarf dress appeared – made from four Gucci signature scarves, highlighting the royally-endorsed floral and insect motifs.

A year earlier, the Gucci 'dream-come-true' outlet opened in the family's native Florence. Situated on the Via Tornabuoni, the city's most elegant and luxurious thoroughfare, the store was elegance and style personified with a huge glass and bronze door leading into an interior carpeted in a lush green weave, walled with walnut and glass cabinets, and lit by eight magnificent chandeliers made of Murano glass and Florentine bronze. There was also a leather-lined lift, featuring the famous Gucci red and green stripe. Employees at this store were the first to wear uniforms - white shirt, black jacket, tie and black/grey striped trousers for men while the saleswomen wore three piece burgundy suits in winter, substituting with a similar beige-coloured combination during the warmer months. Neither male nor female employees wore 'horsebit loafers' as it was not deemed appropriate for employees to sport the same footwear as the well-heeled clientele. The opening of this flagship store was delayed by the River Arno bursting its banks and flooding the premises, although miraculously 90% of the stock was salvaged. Meanwhile, away from the city centre, a new 150,000 square foot factory was constructed which would house design, production, and storage facilities.

Further new lines followed in 1969 with Aldo reworking the Diamante print to include further use of the double G logo. A complete range of luggage was developed with this fabric and a pigskin trim, with additions of a cosmetic case for ladies and a toilet case for

ABOVE: The changing of the Diamante print
RIGHT: Gucci Store, Via Tornabuoni, Florence, Italy, 1969

GUCCI

and skirt set made from suede and clipped together with stylish clasps. The fashion press applauded the range, in particular a black leather raincoat with sleeves extending straight from the collar, a wide belt of blue and red canvas, and a matching handbag. Jewellery and gem-enhanced watches were also on display. All-in-all, there were 2000 different products – heralding a massive growth of items.

The early 1970s saw further expansion in both stores and products. Shops opened in Tokyo, Hong Kong and the United Arab Emirates while the first Gucci fragrance – 'Gucci No 1 for Women' launched in 1974. With notes of aldehydes, rose, amber and bergamot, it was an instant success. This same year the Gucci Model 2000L Watch saw the light of day. Made in Switzerland with Swiss quartz, black face and a gold

gentlemen. At the launch, models of both sexes were sent down the runway in outfits made from the same fabric which resulted in gasps of delight and a standing ovation from the audience. The first Gucci ready-to-wear women's collection was launched this same year. Sporty and casual yet impeccably stylish and beautifully made, it was Aldo's aim for Gucci to be worn in everyday settings rather than at exclusive, black-tie events. The garments included a tweed trouser suit in pale gold with the tunic top featuring a soft, glove leather bandeau; a maxi dinner skirt in leather with fox-fur hem trim and matching braces; short sporty skirts and shift dresses; and a bra

ABOVE: Gucci Model 2000L Watch
ABOVE RIGHT: Gucci No 1 for Women
OPP PAGE: AMC Gucci Hornet

HORNET SPORTABOUT.
Every woman knows her compact does two things:
It looks good. And it carries things that make her look good.
So when we designed our compact for women, we did the same.
We made a sporty car – that carries things.
Our compact is easy to handle. It's less than 15 feet long and has a turning circle as small as a VW Beetle.
And our compact handles packages easily. The rear seat folds down. And the top-hinged liftgate is fully counter-balanced to open easily.
For the interior, we went all the way.
All the way to Italy.
With love, a world-famous designer played red against dark green against ivory to perfection.
The result is the Gucci interior, a very special option.
For any woman who's looking for a car, we suggest she take a look at herself in our compact.

Counter clockwise from top: Hornet Sportabout "X" in Skyway Blue, Sportabout "D/L" in Butterscotch Gold, and Sportabout in Hunter Green, metallic.

Gucci-designed interior, optional. Green vinyl reclining seats, trimmed in ivory and red. Carpeting: dark green. Headliner: Ivory and green with double-G pattern.

HORNET IS BACKED BY THE AMERICAN MOTORS BUYER PROTECTION PLAN.

case, the classic timepiece went on to sell a million units in two years, setting a new world record. The '70s also brought expansion in the areas of luxury product design and bespoke commissions. Appealing to uber-wealthy travellers, the Gucci 'Rolls Royce' luggage set was launched in 1970. A year later, the brand linked up with the American Motor Company to produce the 'Gucci Hornet', the classic Hornet car featuring a classic leather Gucci interior.

La Casa Gucci was flying high but there were storm clouds on the horizon. The family in-fighting that was to follow – and the serious repercussions this would have on the brand and business - would have had founder Guccio Gucci turning in his grave. . .

ABOVE: Gucci advert from the 1970s
RIGHT: Gucci advert from the 1980s

GUCCI
Firenze·Roma·Milano·Montecatini·Parigi·Londra·New York·Palm Beach·Bal Harbour Fla·Beverly Hills·Chicago·Hong Kong·27 Old Bond Street London W1X 3AA 01-629 2716

FAMILY AT WAR

'Bishero! You are fired! You are an idiot to try to compete with us! A fantastic idiot! I cannot protect you anymore'

Aldo Gucci to his 'young pretender' son Paolo

In 1974, Vasco Gucci passed away childless. His widow sold her shares to the two remaining brothers with the company then being split 50-50 between Aldo and Rodolfo. Aldo gave each of his three sons 3.3%, leaving him with 40% while his brother retained 50%. Despite the imbalance, Aldo maintained control of the company and kept it stable and profitable during his reign – at least to begin with. The brothers had their differences but Aldo and Rodolfo managed to get along most of the time – although it was Aldo who called the shots as he always had done.

It wasn't until their children became heavily involved in the 1970s that the problems at Gucci really started. The biggest troublemaker was one of Aldo's three sons, Paolo. While one of the most creative members of the Gucci clan, he was also the most difficult to work with. Paolo locked horns with both his father and his uncle. He wanted to start an entirely new designer label within the company, one with its own stores and targeted at a much younger demographic. Aldo and Rodolfo refused to agree to this before demoting him into a small role within the business. Paolo rebelled and in 1980, secretly launched his own designer label under the name 'Paolo Gucci' which was largely inspired by the 1966 'Flora' print. He had big plans for the label, and dreamed of designing *'lamps, sunglasses, furniture, sleepwear, bedding accessories and fabrics, wall coverings, ladies' underwear, lingerie, plates and flatware.'* However, on discovering Paolo's clandestine plans, Rodolfo and Aldo fired him before suing to block him from using the Gucci name in any business pursuits of his own. Meanwhile Gucci Galliera, described by Aldo as *'a cultural concept in retailing'* with the aim of catering solely to the elite, opened in New York City. VIPs were given 18k gold keys for the elevator in order to whisk them up to the exclusive fourth floor.

'The celebrated double-G has come to represent more than success,' observed publication 'The Age'; *'Gucci means prestige and good taste.'*

A classic Horsebit loafer also went on display at New York's Metropolitan Museum of Art.

However, problems within the family began to escalate. Paolo may not have worked at Gucci any more but he still owned a 3.3% stake in the business. He was thus entitled to attend board meetings and

RIGHT: Paolo Gucci

question all manner of company dealings, such as Aldo's questionable handling of finances over the years which included Gucci Snr sticking his fingers into the till to the tune of millions of dollars. Hugely resentful of his father, in 1982 Paolo filed documents in the US courts that laid bare how Aldo had cheated the government out of seven million dollars in taxes between the years of 1977 to 1982. The Internal Revenue Service began its investigation and in January 1986, Aldo Gucci pleaded guilty to one count of conspiracy and two counts of fraud in a scheme involving sham foreign corporations, false billing procedures and the diversion to personal use of funds intended for business purposes. Aldo was found guilty and served a year in federal prison for tax evasion.

'I feel very sorry, deeply sorry for what happened, for what I have done,' Aldo confessed in court.

This, however, was not the only humiliation Aldo had suffered courtesy of his son. Though Aldo owned a 40% stake in Gucci compared with his brother's 50%, throughout the early 1980s he still ran the business as if he were the major share-holder. He knew that so long as his brother Rodolfo was alive, he would never have to worry about losing control of the company. But when Rodolfo passed away in May 1983 aged 71, his 50% stake was inherited by his only son, Maurizio. Like his cousin Paolo, Maurizio wanted to make changes at Gucci. He teamed up with Paolo in the hope of taking control of the company. In the summer of 1984, Maurizio and Paolo came to an agreement.

ABOVE: Paolo, Aldo and Rodolfo, opening of the Old Bond Street store, in London, March 22, 1977
LEFT: Aldo Gucci in Palm Beach, Florida, 1974

Paolo would vote his shares with Maurizio's, enabling him to take control of Gucci. In return, Maurizio promised he would buy out his cousin's 3.3% stake for $22 million, thus giving Paolo the finances required to bankroll his own designer-goods company. The following September, the cousins put their plan into action, stripping Aldo of his power. They offered to let him stay on in a figurehead role, but when Aldo tried to fight back, he was thrown out of the company entirely. He did, however, still have a 40% stake.

Maurizio and Paolo's deal fell apart just two months later, before Maurizio could get his hands on Paolo's shares. Paolo turned Maurizio in to the Italian authorities for cheating on inheritance taxes, forcing Maurizio to flee to Switzerland to avoid arrest. Maurizio managed to clear up his tax problems without going to jail, but Aldo, Paolo, and Paolo's brothers continued to fight him for control of the company. Meanwhile the Gucci brand was losing its elite, exclusive cachet and image. The first ready-to-wear 'Flora' pattern-inspired Gucci fashion show had been held in Florence in 1981 and deemed a great success but while the company made big profits in the early 1980s, it lost a great deal in the process. Thanks to the huge success of Gucci's cheaper, mass-marketed line of leather-and-canvas bags, sold not just in Gucci's boutiques but in almost any retail store willing to stock them, the brand lost its exclusivity and kudos. Gucci bags were now the kind of fashion items that simply anyone could buy at

ABOVE: Roberto, Giorgio and Maurizio Gucci at a new store of Gucci in Paris, 1983
RIGHT: Paul Poiret

all manner of retail outlets. The halcyon days of the brand being patronised by the likes of Jackie Kennedy Onassis and Princess Grace were long gone. By the late 1980s, Gucci was seen as tacky and tasteless. Having returned to Italy, Maurizio wanted to restore Gucci's faded lustre. He was convinced that the only way he would be able to achieve this was by having a free hand and total control of the company. Therefore, he needed to buy out his relatives. He did not have the means to achieve this himself. The only option open to him was to find an outside investor. In 1987 Investcorp, a Bahraini investment bank, agreed to buy the shares. Paolo sold out first, followed by his brothers, and then finally Aldo, who sold his shares in April 1989, nine months before his death in January 1990.

Guccio Gucci's grandsons, Paolo and Maurizio, now had the means to pursue their dreams. Maurizio was finally free to run Gucci as he saw fit while Paolo had the money he needed to get his own designer label off the ground. Neither cousin fared well. Paolo was the first to fail. Through a combination of high living and incompetent business decisions, he managed to burn through $40 million of his own money without ever opening for business. In 1993, he filed for bankruptcy, so broke that he couldn't even pay his phone bill, let alone find the more than $350,000 in back alimony and child support he owed his ex-wife. When he died from liver failure in 1995 at the age of 64, the Gucci company bought the rights to his name from the bankruptcy court.

Maurizio's fate was even worse. His instincts about returning Gucci to its glory days were good, but he killed off many of the company's most profitable product lines before there was anything new to replace them with. Its boutique stores empty of customers and its coffers haemorrhaging cash, by the dawn of the 1990s, Gucci had a negative net worth of $17.3 million and was losing $30 million a year. The brand desperately needed a revival strategy to prevent itself from becoming history. Thus in 1990, Dawn Mello, president of Bergdorf Goodman, was appointed creative director, executive vice president and chief designer of Gucci. Ms Mello had form saving fashion houses that found themselves in trouble. She had revitalised Bergdorf Goodman in the 1980s and it was profoundly hoped that she would work the same miracle for Gucci. Ms Mello immediately set to work, reducing the number of Gucci stores from over a thousand to just 180 in a bid to rebuild the brand's exclusivity. She also axed the number of items sold by Gucci from 22,000 to 7,000, and, by appointing Florentine artisans to renovate, tone down and update products, she revived the iconic Bamboo bag and the Gucci loafer. By doing this, she was able to begin to restore Gucci's 'A' list cachet, lustre and aura of exclusivity. 'The New York Times' reported that Mello's Fall 1990 line-up *'looks a lot like the old Gucci, circa the 1960's'*. But she had still to play her ace card. This was to hire a young, then unknown, Texan designer called Tom Ford to take up the position of head women's ready-to-wear designer. . .

RIGHT: Dawn Mello

THE TOM FORD YEARS

'The Gucci woman – you know what she's after'

Tom Ford

Thomas Carlyle Ford didn't study fashion design. In 1985 aged 24, he graduated from the Parsons School of Design in New York City with a degree in interior architecture. However, fashion had long been a passion. As a student he would spend his nights at the legendary 'Studio 54' in New York where he met Andy Warhol and the glamorous likes of Halston, Bianca Jagger and Jerry Hall. The club's disco-era glamour would influence his future fashion creations, with the characters who frequented '54' being a constant source of innovation and inspiration. After each visit, he would rush to a nearby cafeteria and draw fashion sketches of the louche, often outrageous and overtly sexy looks he had seen there.

ABOVE: Legendary logo of Studio 54
RIGHT: Rupert Smith, Cindy, Tom Ford, and Ian Falconer going to Studio 54. 1980

Following graduation, Ford worked for a year in the 'Chloe' press office in Paris and on returning to the US, he called American designer Cathy Hardwick every day for a month in hopes of securing a job at her sportswear company. Hardwick eventually agreed to interview him.

'I'd had every intention of giving him no hope,' she was to later recall. *'But then I asked him who his favourite European designers were. He said, "Armani" and "Chanel". Months later I asked him why he said that, and he said, "Because you were wearing Armani". Is it any wonder he got the job?'*

Ford worked as a design assistant for Hardwick for two years before landing a job designing jeans for Perry Ellis on New York's Seventh Avenue, but he had his eyes on a bigger prize.

'If I was ever going to become a good designer, I had to leave America,' he was later to say. *'My own culture was inhibiting me. Too much style in America is tacky. It's looked down upon to be too stylish. Europeans, however, appreciate style.'*

The fashion gods must have read his thoughts. Gucci were at an all-time low with Dawn Mello later recalling that at the time, *'no one would dream of wearing Gucci'*. She approached Ford, although didn't hold out much hope that he would be willing to relocate to Milan.

'I was talking to a lot of people, and most didn't want the job,' Mello said. *'For an American designer to move to Italy to join a company that was far from being a premium brand was pretty risky.'*

It was a risk that Ford was willing to take. He joined the company in 1990 as the brand's chief women's ready-to-wear designer but his role at Gucci rapidly expanded. He was designing menswear within six months and shoes soon after that. He was made design director in 1992, heading up the brand's ready-to-wear lines, fragrances, image, advertising and store design. By 1993, Ford was in charge of designing 11 product lines and putting in 18-hour days. However, there was tension between Ford and Maurizio Gucci who at this time was still chairman with a 50% stake in the company.

'Maurizio always wanted everything to be round and brown, and Tom wanted to make it square and black,' Dawn Mello recalled.

Though Maurizio Gucci wanted to fire Ford on more than one occasion, Mello and Gucci CEO Domenico De Sole insisted that he remain. Nonetheless, Ford's work during the early 1990s was primarily behind the scenes. By 1993, it was clear that Maurizio Gucci could no longer be chairman of the company. He had racked up $40 million in personal debts at the same time that he was running the company into the ground. Maurizio had used his Gucci shares as collateral for personal loans. With the company still

LEFT C-WISE, FROM TOP: Fashion designer Loulou de la Falaise with Andy Warhol and Halston; Jerry Hall and Truman Capote; Bianca Jagger, all in Studio 54

bleeding money despite the arrival of Mello and Ford, Maurizio had no income and no means of paying off his debts. Investcorp was the only thing keeping the company afloat but it had long since lost faith in Maurizio's abilities. No surprises there. Maurizio lost over US$22 million in 1993 alone. Investcorp refused to pump any more money into Gucci until he was gone. The company was less than 48 days away from closing its doors and having its assets sold at auction when Maurizio, himself nearly bankrupt for non-payment of personal debts, gave up the fight and sold his 50% stake to Investcorp. For the first time, there were no Guccis at Gucci. There never would be again.

It wasn't until Maurizio had been forced out of the company that Ford's Midas-touch and creative genius slowly began to come to the fore. In 1994, Dawn Mello returned to Bergdorf Goodman in New York, and Ford was appointed Gucci's creative director. For his 1994 debut women's collection, Gucci's publicist had trouble getting fashion journalists to even show up. Still under the influence of what Maurizio Gucci had wanted, i.e pastel shades and soft knits, the collection was a flop and Ford was close to quitting immediately afterwards. But then fate, yet again, played a part. In March 1995, Maurizio was murdered by a hitman later discovered to have been hired by his estranged first wife Patricia, played by Lady Gaga in the 2021 movie 'House of Gucci'. With

ABOVE: Gucci executive Dawn Mello, Tom Ford, with guests at the Handbag Production Facility, in Milan
RIGHT: Dame Anna Wintour

the world's attention focusing on the tragedy, Ford – although obviously saddened by the killing of his former boss - took the opportunity to go under the radar and design the kind of collection he wanted.

'Nobody was worried about what the product was going to be," Ford later said. *"The business was in such bad shape that nobody really gave the merchandise a thought. I was left with a completely open door.'*

What emerged was a collection that oozed sex appeal. Grunge and minimalism had dominated women's wear trends for several years and Ford's instinct was that women wanted to look sexy again. He was right. His 1995 Autumn/Winter collection showcased a range of Halston-inspired hip-hugging velvet bell bottomed trousers, skin-tigh satin shirts and mohair jackets in jewel-like hues, sleek suits, and car-finish metallic patent boots. Modelled by the likes of Kate Moss, Helena Christensen and Amber Valletta, the fashion show was an unapologetically flash package of runway sex appeal. The collection was edgy, sexy, feminine and, most importantly, trendy. When the show was over, Ford took his rebellion one step further by ignoring the clause in his contract that forbade him from taking a bow at the end of the show.

'I had so much pent-up energy,' Ford was to recall. *'I had never been allowed to walk out on the runway when Maurizio and Dawn were still there – I just decided that this was my chance. I didn't ask anyone's permission. I had done the show, designed the clothes that I felt were right, and I just walked right out there. Sometimes in life you have to take things if you want to move forward. The next day, I couldn't even get in the showroom. It was absolute hysteria. No one gave me flak after that.'*

For Dame Anna Wintour, Vogue legend and high priestess of all things high fashion, the show was a pivotal moment.

'When I think back to the early '90s, fashion was buried deep in the shapeless layers of the horrible grunge look. Along came Tom with his low-cut hipsters and grunge was sent scurrying back off to Seattle,' she said.

ABOVE & RIGHT: Gucci Ready to Wear Spring Summer show as part of the Milan fashion week, October 04, 1995

ABOVE & RIGHT: Gucci Ready to Wear Spring Summer show as part of the Milan fashion week, October 04, 1995

ABOVE & RIGHT: Gucci 90s adverts following Tom Ford's "Sex Sells" ethos

GUCCI
london • 33 old bond street • 18 sloane street • harrods • room of luxury

Joan Kaner, senior vice president and fashion director for luxury US store Neiman Marcus agreed.

'It was hot! It was sex!' she recalled. *'The girls looked like they had stepped off someone's private jet. You just knew that wearing those clothes would make you look like you were living on the edge – doing it and having it all.'*

The fashion press was equally effusive.

'The effortlessly sexuality of it all had a chill factor that just froze the audience to their seats,' wrote Harper's Bazaar.

Ford – hailed by the New York Times as the 'new Karl Lagerfeld' with reference to how that German designer had turned around the fortunes of Chanel in the 1980s - brought in French stylist Carine Roitfeld and photographer Mario Testino to create a series of scandalously stunning advertisement campaigns for this new-look Gucci. So provocative were some of the images that the ads would go on to be banned in some countries. Meanwhile 'A' listers including Madonna, Gwyneth Paltrow and Elizabeth Hurley picked up on the Ford factor at Gucci from the get-go. It wasn't until the 1996 autumn/winter show, however, that Ford introduced some of his iconic motifs that would remain consistent throughout his 10-year reign as King of Gucci. He was quoted saying that this was the show where *'it all came together for the first time'*.

Moving away from the previous year's explosion of disco-inspired colours, this collection featured slinky white cut-out dresses accessorised with gold belt buckles or gold 'horse-bit' belts and fastenings on the peep holes; velvet, wide-lapelled tuxedos in red and midnight blue; and oversized furs and chic pinstripes. Ford's signature hip-hugging bell bottoms and slashed-to-the naval, second skin-like satin shirts also featured. For the show, he killed the back light and put a spotlight on each model going down the catwalk. This was to focus all of the attention on the looks and to stop the audience from becoming distracted by seeing one from another across the runway. Accompanied by a sensual soundtrack, the effect was like being in the coolest nightclub on the planet. Vogue's description couldn't have been more accurate, describing the experience as being the 'equivalent of a one-night-stand at Studio 54'. Business-wise, the Ford factor was proving to be as successful as the fashion. As early as 1995, Gucci's sales spiked with revenues of US$500 million.

ABOVE: Gucci Spring 1997 Menswear Collection
ABOVE: Tom Ford at the end of the Gucci Spring 1997 Menswear Collection Runway Show

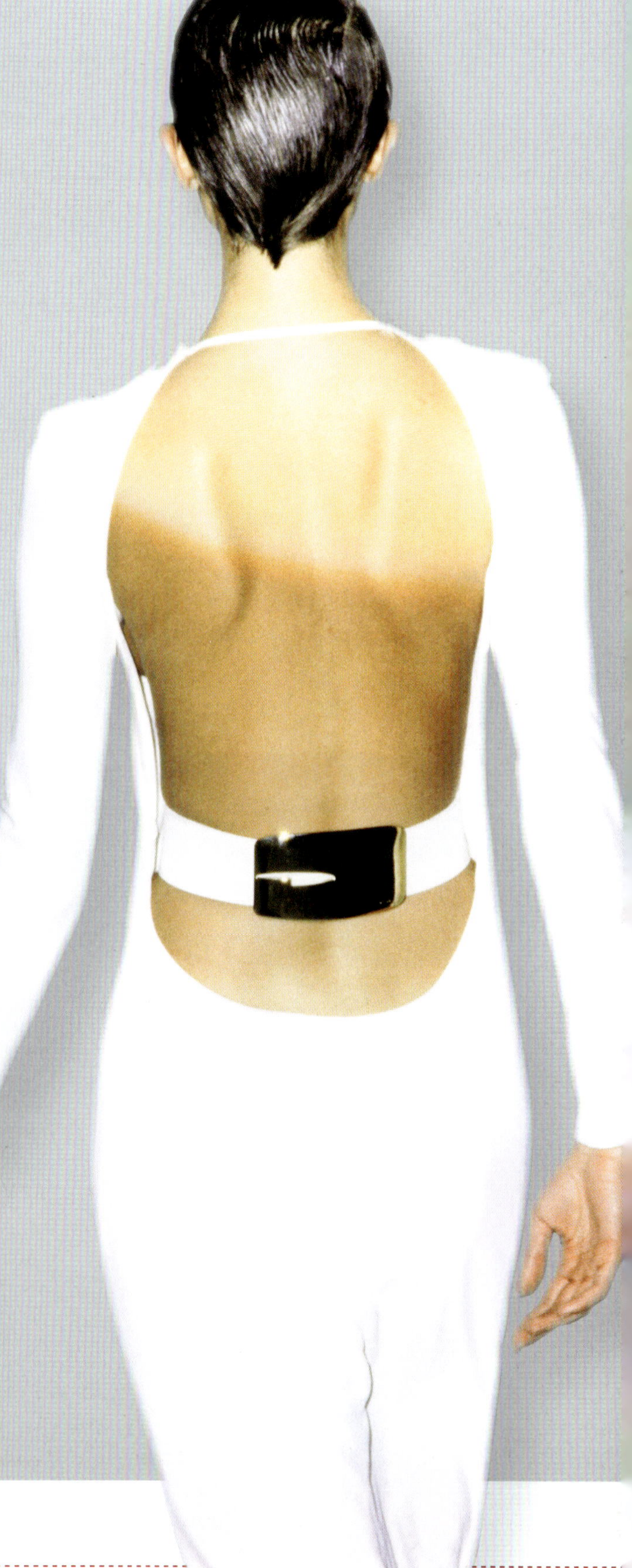

As the 1990s progressed, Ford's designs became even more risqué. Skirts became shorter, heels became higher. Highlights included the famous Gucci G-string – a piece of skimpy underwear held together by the iconic Gucci logo fashioned in metal – and worn on the catwalk by both male and female models.

'Fifteen minutes in came the infamous, interlocking G-logo G-string, styled with an open-knit sweater, a shoulder bag and ankle boots – the model's hair damp, as though she had just stepped out of a Bel-Air swimming pool, her eyes daubed in smoky, morning-after-the-night-before make-up; a spotlight bathing her bare cheeks in a music-video glow,' wrote Vogue magazine of a Gucci 1997 fashion show. *'Next off the starting blocks: a mens' version, worn by runway model Sacha, who (luckily for us) had a free moment to walk reporters through his look backstage: "There's a little pad up front, but in the back you've got nothing but a string, baby!".'*

ABOVE: The famous Gucci G-string
RIGHT: Gucci Fall 1996 Ready to Wear Runway Show
OPP. PAGE: Tom Ford and Kate Moss backstage at Gucci Spring 1996 Ready to Wear show

A less controversial Ford classic proved to be his skinny, hip-skimming belt which also featured the famous double G logo.

When Gucci acquired the House of Yves Saint Laurent (YSL) in 1999, Ford was named Creative Director of that label as well. Saint Laurent himself was not happy and failed to hide his displeasure with Ford's overtly sexy designs for the ready-to-wear line. *'The poor man does what he can,'* was his verdict. During his time as creative director for YSL, Ford nonetheless won numerous Council of Fashion Designers of America Awards and was able to pull the classic fashion house back into the mainstream. His advertising campaigns for the YSL fragrance Opium with model Sophie Dahl wearing only a necklace and stiletto heels in a

ABOVE: Sophie Dahl YSL advert for Opium
TOP: Gucci Skinny belt
OPP. PAGE: Gucci Ready to Wear Fall/Winter 2001

sexually suggestive pose caused controversy – as did the campaign for YSL M7 cologne which featured martial arts champion Samuel de Cubber in full frontal nudity. However, Ford would tell Vogue France some years later that he was not *'into gratuitous provocation'*. He defended his campaign by saying: *'When I decided to show a full-frontal male nude as the face of M7 fragrance, I was defending sexual equality. I believe we live in a culture that objectifies women, but as soon as it's a man on show, there's a real phobia and everyone's outraged.'*

Eyebrows were certainly raised in 2003 when, for a Gucci advertising campaign, a female model was photographed half-naked with the outline of the Gucci 'G' logo shaved into her pubic hair. Ford is said to have carried out the task himself and then perfected the shape with an eyebrow pencil! This was another Ford/Testino/Roitfeld production whose success was in little doubt. According to Vogue, the year after this power trio began working together on campaigns, Gucci's sales increased by 90%. Proof yet again that sex sells.

By the late 1990s, Ford had started to give a nod to Gucci's former glory days by introducing more classic styles but these still featured signature 'Fordisms' of figure-hugging designs with flesh a-plenty on display. Less controversial was Ford's relaunch of the iconic 'Jackie' bag during 1999 and 2000 to great acclaim and popularity. Using a variety of materials and shades, the bag once again became 'the' handbag to have – just as it had been years before.

www.gucci.com

ABOVE: The infamous 2003 Gucci advert

By the end of the century, Gucci, almost bankrupt less than 10 years earlier, was in the black to the tune of $4billion and once again synonymous with high-end fashion and luxury. It was at this time that Gucci changed hands and was bought by François Pinault's Kering group which still owns the company to this day in addition to other fellow luxury brands Balenciaga, Alexander McQueen, Bottega Veneta, and Stella McCartney.

Ford's Gucci highlights of the late eighties and early noughties included a shimmering lilac, halter-neck, asymmetric dress , bondage-style bikini top, a fringed metallic evening bag with emerald green serpent clasp, python-print cutaway swimsuit, crystal-decorated harem pants, the iconic Gucci trim presented in different colour ways to the standard green/red combo, and the matching leather combos modelled by David and Victoria Beckham in 1999. The Spring/Summer 2001 collection ranks among Ford's great coups at Gucci. Filled with satin shirts, billowing trousers, eclectic prints, and unconventional suiting, it offers a snapshot of the Ford era at Gucci - bad boy luxury, oozing sexuality and challenging the industry's status quo. Clair Watson, couture director at Doyle New York, an Upper East Side auction house, perfectly understood Ford's popularity at Gucci. *'The early years of this century were all about sex in the abstract, and Tom Ford mastered the "about to have sex" look at Gucci,'* she told New York magazine.

It was expected that Ford would become the brand's CEO in 2006 but in a shock move, in April 2004 he announced he was leaving Gucci. It is said

he felt unable to meet the demands of one of the conglomerate's biggest shareholders. The divorce between the designer and the conglomerate led to an ugly fallout with public accusations coming from both sides while sordid details were relished by the press. Later, in an interview with 'Women's Wear Daily' Ford said, '*Money had absolutely nothing to do with it at all. It really was a question of control.*' He has since referred to this experience as '*devastating*' and a '*midlife crisis*'.

'*It's so sad for me,*' he said. '*I went through a really tough sort of depression, which I think is normal. It was 14 years of my life.*'

It was certainly the end of an era.

'*This changes the landscape,*' said Glenda Bailey, then editor of Harper's Bazaar. '*Someone on the staff said to me, "You know, it's like the end of the '90s now. Everything will change." I've called Tom "the Prince Charming of Fashion" because he came along, he kissed Gucci and all the sudden, she went to the ball – and wearing the most beautiful shoes!*'

ABOVE: Tom Ford aknowledges applauses at the end of his last Gucci collection
LEFT: Gucci 2004 autumn and winter show in Milan

HANA
ELISE
DARIA
NATASHA
EUGENIA
TIIU
JULIA
LIYA
RIANNE
MARIACARLA
MIMI
GEMMA
MARIJA
UJJWALA
GEORGINA
DAVID
RYAN
JON

ABOVE & LEFT: Gucci Fall 2004 Ready to Wear Runway Show Backstage preparations

TOM FORD @ GUCCI

His best red-carpet creations

1995

Madonna at the MTV Video Music Awards, 1995. Megastar Madonna wore Tom Ford at Gucci – hip-hugging bell-bottoms and turquoise satin blouse open almost to the navel – to the 1995 MTV Music Awards, thus signalling that it was now the hottest label in the land.

British actress and 'It' girl Elizabeth Hurley in a Gucci white fur coat and patent boots while accompanying then-boyfriend Hugh Grant to the premiere of 'The American President', 1995.

1996

Gwyneth Paltrow in Tom Ford iconic red velvet suit at the MTV VMAs in 1996. Paltrow wore this again in 2021 to attend Gucci's Love Parade celebration.

Nicole Kidman and then husband Tom Cruise at the 'To Die For' Sydney Premiere in 1996 - dressing the most A-List of A-List mid 1990s couples in matching Gucci was quite a coup.

1997

It's 1997, and Jennifer Lopez isn't quite the icon she's about to become but Ford saw her appeal and dressed her in this custom Gucci outfit to attend a benefit dinner he hosted in Los Angeles.

Future Alessandro Michele muse Jared Leto at the AIDS Project Los Angeles Benefit Dinner in 1997. Twenty-four years on, he would play Paolo Gucci in the 2021 biopic 'House of Gucci'.

'Fresh Prince of Bel Air' actress Nia Long in a key look from the spring 1997 collection at the AIDS Project Los Angeles Benefit Dinner in 1997.

1998

Helen Hunt wears a baby blue Gucci gown at the Oscars in 1998 to collect her Academy Award for 'As Good As It Gets'.

1999

Madonna at the Grammys in 1999. After her major Gucci moment in 1995, Madonna returned to the label in 1999 in a pair of bedazzled, lilac harem pants and simple white tank.

A brunette Gwyneth Paltrow in snakeskin-print Gucci dress at the Met Gala in 1999

Jennifer Lopez all a-sparkle in Gucci at the Vogue/VH1 Fashion Awards in 1999.

2000

In her music videos and photoshoots, Lil' Kim was constantly in Gucci. For a party for the Wyclef Jean Foundation, she wore a matching top, boots and bag from the fall 2000 collection.

Kate Winslet at the 'Holy Smoke' premiere in 2000 in a pair of the era-defining snakeskin flares Tom Ford sent down Gucci's spring 2000 runway.

2001

US actress Joan Allen in Gucci at the 2001 Independent Spirit Awards in 2001, proving that TF could also turn out a sort of refined casual wear that would turn Ralph Lauren green with envy.

Heather Graham wearing a black baby doll dress from the fall 2001 collection to the Toronto International Film Festival in 2001.

2002

Naomi Watts red carpet appearance at the Oscars

2003

Nicole Kidman rocks a little red Gucci dress at the SAG Awards in 2003

Nicole Kidman at the Goddess-themed Met Gala in 2003 which she co-hosted with Mr F.

Diana Ross wears Gucci and Tom Ford-designed YSL at the Met Gala in 2003.

Sarah Jessica Parker in super-sexy Tom Ford at the Tony Awards in 2003

Halle Berry at Gothika Premiere in 2003, exemplifies the Gucci look of the early '00s in this burnt-orange cocktail dress.

Beyoncé at a party in 2003

2004

Mary J. Blige in neon Gucci at the Grammys in 2004.

(RIGHT) Charlize Theron in a golden Gucci gown to accept her Academy Award at the 2004 Oscars.

GIANNINI'S GUCCI

'Frida Giannini is from a different generation than Milan's other female designers - she sees fashion from a more pragmatic standpoint'

Vogue

Following Tom Ford's dramatic exit, Gucci decided to look in-house rather than hire a well-known name to fill the Texan's starry shoes. Three designers took over – Frida Giannini for accessories, Alessandra Facchinetti for women's wear, and John Ray for men's wear. Facchinetti left after a forgettable two seasons with Ray following shortly after that. The result was that in 2005, Giannini was named as Creative Director for Gucci overall. Born in Rome in 1972, she studied fashion design at the city's prestigious Fashion Academy and briefly worked at a number of small, family-run accessories companies before joining Fendi in 1997 to design ready-to-wear. After three seasons, she was promoted to designer of leather goods with her handbags becoming must-have items. In 2002, she was hired as Gucci's design director of handbags, having been hand-picked for the post by Tom Ford.

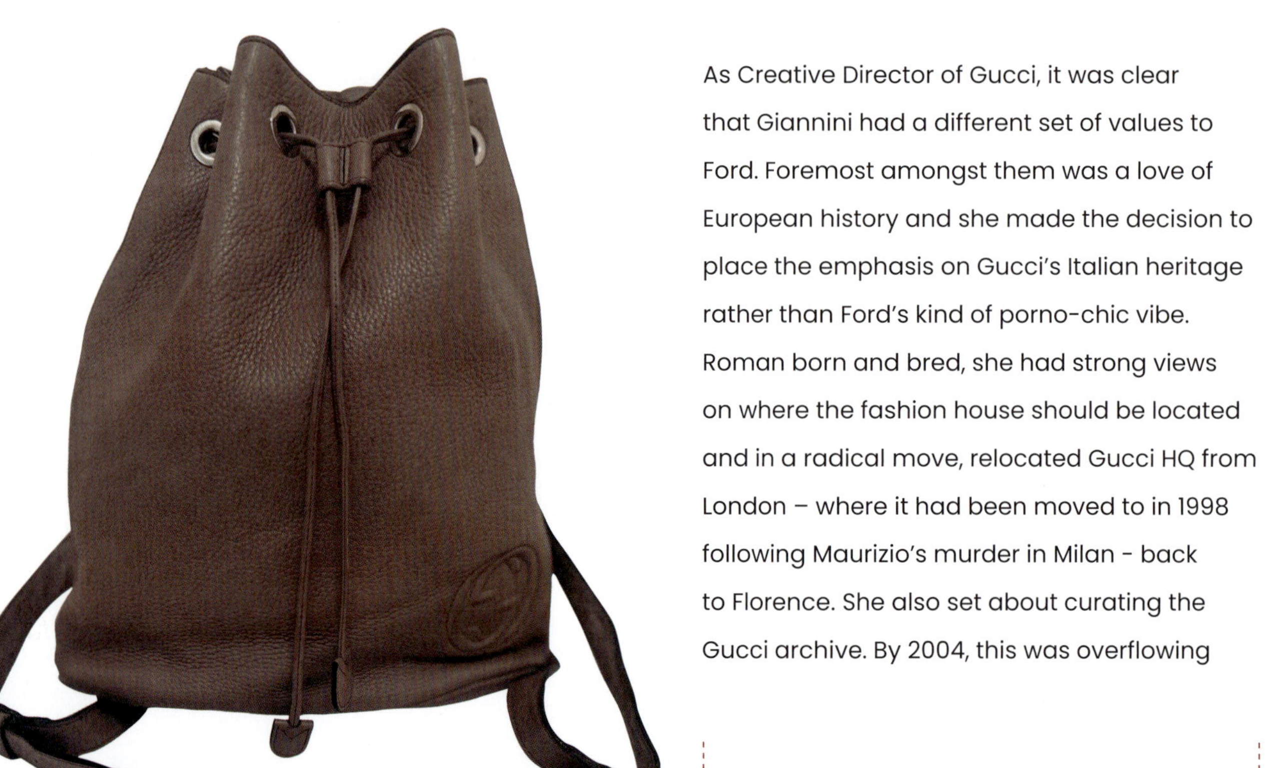

As Creative Director of Gucci, it was clear that Giannini had a different set of values to Ford. Foremost amongst them was a love of European history and she made the decision to place the emphasis on Gucci's Italian heritage rather than Ford's kind of porno-chic vibe. Roman born and bred, she had strong views on where the fashion house should be located and in a radical move, relocated Gucci HQ from London – where it had been moved to in 1998 following Maurizio's murder in Milan - back to Florence. She also set about curating the Gucci archive. By 2004, this was overflowing

LEFT: Frida Giannini's Gucci Soho Backpack
RIGHT: Frida Giannini

ABOVE: Gucci fashion show in Milan, unveiling short jackets and ruffled dresses for Frida Giannini's first women's wear designs, September 27, 2005

with hundreds of forgotten and unused designs. Giannini rediscovered these and took inspiration from them, reviving in 2005 the Flora design – something Tom Ford had constantly refused to do. The revival, under Giannini, however, proved to be hugely successful. In addition, she resurrected the long-dormant Gucci canvas print and the classic red and green equestrian stripe also returned to the heart of Gucci design.

However, it wasn't only in the Gucci archives that Giannini found inspiration. She loved the retro romance of Fellini's 'La Dolce Vita', the androgynous glamour of 1970s David Bowie, the nostalgia of 'Breakfast at Tiffany's', and the ever-changing looks and style of her childhood idol, Madonna.

'*Inspiration for a designer can come from many different sides and directions,*' she once said. '*You can be inspired by a place after a trip, or by an exhibition of art, or from music, or from films. You can also be influenced by an age, like the '60s or '70s. Of course, there are certain rules you have to operate by in terms of markets, and for summer and for winter. But at the end of the day, you are a person. You put a lot of yourself into the clothes.*'

Yet, despite all this, initially the sartorial spectre of Tom Ford continued to loom large

RIGHT: The 'Flora Bag" from Gucci's 2005 cruise accessories collection designed by Frida Giannini
ABOVE: Lily Donaldson, Gucci's spring 2006 show

over Giannini's collections. What started off as a subtle tweak to his signature glam rock aesthetic which showcased '90s metallic accessories, platform shoes with an identical 'car paint' high-shine finish, glitzy gold and purple oversized fur ensembles, and sequin-covered fabrics morphed into identifiable Giannini streetwear collections offset by delicate party dresses, bohemian flounces, tropical-print shirts, and sharply tailored androgynous suits. Giannini moved away from Ford's overt, sexed-up style and more towards classic, pre-Fordian Gucci. As the label celebrated its 85th birthday in 2006, she drew inspiration from the label's Dolce Vita years, saying she had been thinking a lot about the 1960s. By 2007 and 2008, Giannini was starting to find her feet a little more and would go on to focus more on lifestyle, cosmetics (launched 2014), and children's clothing lines (launched 2010) with these taking a more prominent place in the Giannini Gucci canon.

'Frida Giannini is from a different generation than Milan's other female designers,' opined Vogue. *'She sees fashion from a more pragmatic standpoint. Gucci now is a clearly segmented, business-like collection with no pretence of being anything other than hip, immediately understandable clothes from a global audience.'*

ABOVE: Gucci's spring 2010 menswear show at Piazza Oberdan in Milan

Gucci

She was perceived as the quintessential Gucci woman of the time. Impeccably groomed and slim, with long honey-blonde hair, sharply parted at the centre, Frida represented the epitome of a sexy yet understated sophisticated style that favoured fitted black dresses, elegant trousers and silk tops, paired with an iconic pair of Gucci strappy-sandals.

There were, however, problems. Giannini's Gucci was criticised for not possessing a strong enough identity – it was said that from a consumer standpoint, it was hard to pin down a *'Gucci image'* during the decade she led the label. It was also suggested that she changed direction too many times, that she was unpredictable and lacked vision or any kind of big-time 'wow' factor. Season by season there was a continual succession of very different inspirations and themes - from sporty-chic switching to the '80s glam rock, then the '70s gypsies, the '40s with Schiaparelli inspired evening dresses, then the colourful embroidery and prints of Russian folklore, the disco-mood with the launch of ultra-slim pants, the California mood with exotic prints. . . Apart from Giannini's inconsistencies, though, Gucci may have been a victim of their own popularity, with Gucci bootlegs flooding the market and diluting the brand's value. Between 2003 and 2012, a span that included Ford, Giannini, and interim creative directors at the helm, the

LEFT: Gucci Spring Summer 2008 Collection
RIGHT: Gucci's spring 2009 show

brand rested its use of Aldo Gucci's double-G logo. In the United Kingdom, that presented difficulties as trademarks can be rescinded if they aren't used frequently enough over a five-year span. By 2013, the UK Intellectual Property Office deemed that Gucci's trademark was limited to soaps and fragrances —where the logo had figured prominently since 2003— thus allowing companies apart from Gucci to sell clothes and bags bearing the Florentine house's distinctively iconic logo. Considering the abundance of fake goods flooding the market, and the disintegration of the Gucci name, Giannini may have been fighting a losing battle all along.

The Giannini era wasn't without its achievements, however. In 2011, she named Florence Welch of 'Florence and the Machine' as her muse during the Maison's 90th anniversary. Designing a variety of outfits which Welch wore throughout her tours, Giannini produced a riot of unexpected colour and texture which included a collection of aquamarine, scarlet, citrine, burgundy, and violet joined velvet blazers, fur-collared coats, and feather-trimmed fedoras, effortlessly tied together with a traditional Gucci black pencil skirt. The next year saw her curating and overseeing the opening of the Gucci Museum in Florence — a dedicated space intended to showcase not only the Maison's most iconic archival pieces, but also the works of budding contemporary artists. Interestingly, she chose to display few Tom Ford designs. In addition to resurrecting the Flora and the Gucci stripe, she revamped the Bamboo handbag, coined Gucci's signature 'Frida' narrow silhouette and slim-cut trousers, and strategically redesigned each Gucci boutique to facilitate natural light, whilst incorporating warm wood, alongside amber glass fixtures and fittings.

ABOVE: Florence Welch wearing Gucci arrives at the 10th Annual LACMA Art + Film Gala 2021
MAIN IMAGE: Florence Welch performs wearing Gucci dress, Outside Lands Festival, 2018

The collections produced between Spring/Summer 2011 and Spring/Summer 2013 marked Giannini's best years at Gucci. She experimented with bold colour blocking, safari styles and harem pants for SS/2011, moving though to 1970s' inspired fedora hats, fox stoles, python bags and layers of co-ordinating garments for fall-winter. The next year, inspiration largely came from art deco aesthetics with the architecture of historic skyscrapers of New York reproduced on lamé flapper dresses of the jazz era. Fall/Winter 2012 is regarded as perhaps Giannini's most stunning collection – pale-skinned, flame-haired, scarlet-lipped pre-Raphaelite women wrapped in velvet, jacquard or damask robes. In 2013, Giannini's Gucci unveiled a capsule collection with stylish Italian automobile-heir-turned-playboy Lapo Elkann. Lapo's Wardrobe, as the collection was dubbed, was unveiled to christen Gucci's debut menswear store on Milan's Via Brera. The partnership with Elkann was a play towards two markets at once. Firstly, he was an heir to the Fiat fortune and symbolic of Italian wealth, class, and a love of classical tailoring. Secondly, his love for partying and stylish, exuberant outfits made him extremely popular among menswear-inclined internet users. Lapo's Wardrobe was thus used to seek out customers in both the traditional luxury demographic, and emerging customers that were the future of the industry.

Giannini's time at Gucci will be remembered not only for its fashion, but also its philanthropy. In 2005, the house launched an initiative with Unicef, a charity they have continued to support year on year with limited edition pieces and collaborations.

'The primary essence of the Gucci woman is to be very strong and independent,' Giannini said, a sentiment that saw her being committed to the empowerment of women worldwide.

MAIN IMAGE & INSET: Gucci Fashion Show during Milan fashion week Womenswear Autumn/Winter 2011

ABOVE: Gucci's spring 2011 show

ABOVE & LEFT: Gucci Spring 2013, during fashion week in Milan

In 2013, Gucci revealed 'Chime for Change', a global campaign to support women and girls, for which they put on a concert in London featuring Florence Welch, Beyonce and Jay Z. Speaking to Dazed magazine, Giannini explained the motivation behind her charitable focus.

'Gucci has an incredible visibility and a very high profile around the world. Using this visibility to help children in need continues to be extremely important to me.'

Despite the high-profile good works and, on occasion, truly inspirational and visually stunning designs, the wheels were beginning to come off Giannini's Gucci. Her vintage vision and heritage bias were no longer cutting it and profits were down. In late 2014, Giannini and Patrizio Di Marco – the group's CEO and Frida's real-life partner - were fired. Promises were made for Giannini to stay on through 2015—to ensure that the collections shown in early 2015 had a coherent direction—but that idea unravelled in January 2015, when Giannini suddenly left, leaving Gucci in the lurch a few weeks before the brand's Fall/ Winter 15 collection was to be unveiled at Milan Fashion Week. It was left to Giannini's flamboyant deputy and head accessories designer Alessandro Michele to pick up the pieces. . .

LEFT & RIGHT: Gucci Runway, Milan Fashion Week Womenswear Autumn/Winter 2014

ABOVE & LEFT: Gucci magazine adverts from 2014

GUCCI GARDEN & GUCCI COSMOS

A Museum Piece

Housed inside Florence's 14th century palazzo della Mercanzia, the Gucci museum – later renamed as the Gucci Garden – was opened during Frida Giannini's watch as Creative Director. She wanted to create a 'sleek and streamlined space' that would reflect the brand's sartorial values. The 2011 opening coincided with La Casa Gucci's 90th birthday celebrations. From the outside, the building looks like many other medieval buildings in Florence – but with a pink 'Gucci' banner hanging on the frontage. Inside, is nothing less than a Gucci wonderland. Alessandro Michele, Gianniani's successor, took it upon himself to restyle and rename the museum – thus it became the much more attractively dubbed 'Gucci Garden' in January 2018. An apt renaming taking into consideration the brand's historic connection to nature.

Unlike most museums with written explanations of each artwork, the Gucci pieces speak for themselves. There is a three-story chronological structure to the museum that highlights the evolution of Gucci fashion since its creation in 1921. This features pieces such as suitcases from the 1930s, bold floral prints from the 1950s, and tricolored enamel necklaces from the 1970s. The museum showcases a range of iconic pieces, from scarves to luggage to Hilary Swank's iconic dress from the 2011 Academy Awards. Under Giannini's tenure, very

ABOVE: Outside Gucci Garden, Florence
ABOVE RIGHT: Display inside Gucci Garden, Florence

little Tom Ford @ Gucci was on display but Michele created a dedicated Tom Ford section, so inspired was he by the Texan's work while at Gucci. This section is composed of two rooms: one for his ready-to-wear clothes and one for accessories. The clothing room features some of Ford's iconic looks, with a deep magenta colour around the entire room and on the faceless mannequins, the vivid white pieces. The accessories room features a range of pink and red hues with Ford's GG-themed accessories such as the famous g-string, dog collar, and handcuffs.

Aside from this exhibit, Gucci's maximalism is present throughout the rest of the museum. Alessandro Michele's style allowed for more funky looks such as bizarre patterns, gender-neutral shapes, bright colours, and a lot of ruffles. Modern Gucci fashion also is known for its use of flora and fauna prints and detailing such as snakes, bees, flowers, tigers, and zebras. Whether Sabato de Sarno puts his individual stamp on the garden remains to be seen.

Gucci Garden also houses a One Star Michelin restaurant, the 50-seat 'Gucci Osteria'. The two-toned plush green interior creates a dynamic yet relaxing environment. Massimo Bottura, a chef who was awarded three Michelin stars and owns a top-five restaurant in the world, created

the menu. While this menu is not the most economical – it is Gucci after all – those who come to the restaurant to eat, also get a free ticket to the museum.

It goes without saying that Gucci Garden boasts a Gucci Store. The boutique stocks all the latest Gucci fashions and accessories plus it doubles as the museum gift shop – surely the most glamorous of its kind in the world. In addition to the fashion and homeware, also on sale are smaller items like notebooks, pencils, and surprisingly affordable branded paperweights.

Gucci on Tour

Two thousand and twenty-three saw the launch of Gucci Cosmos, a touring exhibition of the House's most iconic designs from its history. Gucci Cosmos explores how for over a century Gucci's abiding codes and spirit have been brought to life in its most iconic designs, and how these era-defining classics have forever inspired and been reinterpreted by the House's design visionaries. The exhibition showcases how this progressive belief in the power of creativity, anchored in the finest Italian craftsmanship and tradition.

Conceived and designed by renowned British contemporary artist Es Devlin and curated by eminent Italian fashion theorist and critic Maria Luisa Frisa, this voyage through Gucci's past, present and future is experienced across eight exhibition 'worlds' that draw together treasures – many previously unseen – from the Gucci Archive. Each world traces a different aspect of Gucci, its unwavering principles since its foundation in 1921, and its ever-renewed inspirations and creativity – from the nascent ambitions of founder Guccio Gucci to the pioneering spirit of his sons Aldo and Rodolfo, and the wildly imaginative powers of more recent creative directors Tom Ford, Frida Giannini, and Alessandro Michele.

Es Devlin, creator of acclaimed installations for

ABOVE: Display in the Gucci Garden exhibition
ABOVE RIGHT: Gucci Cosmos London exhibition advert on the side of a building in east London

prestigious cultural institutions and performances for global recording artists, has fused innovative audio, visual and kinetic technology within Gucci Cosmos. Taking the visual metaphor of orbits within the cosmos, the exhibition conveys the timelessness of Gucci's visionary ethos and how its gravitational pull creates and shifts meaningful dialogues and myriad correspondences between the House's iconic designs, its creatives and artisans, and society at large.

'As a creative endeavour and expression of the times, the house and its history over the past century can be mapped through an ability to evolve and, more broadly, to expand on the mutability of our own consciousness and ability to make cognitive shifts,' she says. 'Rather like a garment itself that is able to be changed and re-tailored, like a shed skin that constantly renews itself.'

Maria Luisa Frisa comments, 'This project was an extraordinary opportunity for me to traverse the universe of Gucci once again and tell its story through the ever-different lens of the clothes, objects, elements, people, and contexts that have made the House an iconic trailblazer within fashion and collective visual culture for over a century. The Gucci Cosmos exhibition is an immersive experience in which the House's origin story and its history are continuously put to the test by the imagination of the future.'

ALESSANDRO MICHELE

'The way you dress is really the way you feel, the way you live, what you read, your choices. That's what I want to put into Gucci'

Alessandro Michele

Like Frida Giannini, Alessandro Michele was a Roman. Born in 1974, he completed his fashion design studies in Rome's Accademia di Costume e di Moda where, in the early 1990s, he learned to design both theatrical costumes and fashion wear. Having graduated, he left the Italian capital for Bologna where he worked for a knitwear company. After three years he moved to Fendi under Karl Lagerfeld's tenure where he worked alongside Frida Giannini and was appointed senior accessories designer, in charge of the company's handbag designs. He joined Gucci in 2002 as an accessories' designer and in 2006, Giannini named him senior designer of Gucci leather goods. In 2011, he was promoted to the position of her associate creative director.

It came as something as a surprise to the world of high fashion when the little-known Michele was named as the new Creative Director of Gucci, following Giannini's departure in very early 2015. Indeed, the wild-haired designer underwent media training before he gave any interviews. If Michele was a shy or reluctant front-man at first, he made an instant impact when it came to his vision for Gucci. In January 2015, he famously had just five days to create the autumn/winter 2016 men's collection with the women's show due to take place a month later.

'We threw away the collection prepared by Frida Giannini and created a show in five days,' said then Gucci president, Marco Bizzarri. *'The only way to communicate our future strategy was via the catwalk show.'*

Michele was responsible for the iconic Double G monogram logo making a re-appearance in belt buckles during those first shows with the new Creative Director going on to feature it on accessories and clothing alongside other Gucci house classics such as the equestrian bit, and red and green stripe.

RIGHT: Alessandro Michele acknowledges the applause of the audience after the Gucci show during Milan Fashion Week Fall/Winter 2016/17

'I saw it as a rebirth of the double G logo,' said Michele shortly afterwards. *'In the past, Gucci has been a bit ashamed of its logo, but it should be proud of it as an emblem of 95 years of history. The logo is an incredible powerful asset for Gucci and it should become as desirable as a leather bag.'*

His first show saw the launch of his soon-to-be famous fur-lined, 'Princetown' loafers complete with the classic horse-bit hardware which signalled his vision to take the label in a more eclectic, eccentric – and gender-neutral - direction. Other highlights from his early shows included male models wearing whimsical pussy-cat bow blouses paired with black trousers and a Gucci belt, military style

TOP: Suede fur-lined 'Princetown' loafers
ABOVE L-R: Jared Leto & Harry Styles
RIGHT: Model wears a pussy-cat bow blouse, Gucci fall 2015 menswear show

colourful coats with fur cuffs, romantic floaty dresses in a botanic print, heirloom rings, and see-through separates. Feedback was positive on the whole which must have come to a relief to Michele.

'I was sure I'd be fired after the first show,' he was to recall.

From the beginning of his tenure, Michele established a pick-and-mix-like aesthetic, selecting for inspiration items from across the decades and in the process, ushering in an era of gender nonconformity while growing a loyal fan base in usually-fickle Hollywood. Michele's singular vision seduced the likes of Jared Leto (a Michele doppelganger), Dakota Johnson, Billie Eilish, and Harry Styles. Michele's muses were a tight-knit group of artists and creatives who perhaps recognised a kindred spirit in him.

In Milan, Michele's initial shows took place at the Diana Majestic, home to Tom Ford and Frida Gianninis collections for the brand, but soon moved to new headquarters on the edge of the city. However, Michele's tenure at Gucci coincided with fashion's newfound penchant for taking pre-season shows on the road, and he stage-directed some never-seen-the-like-before extravaganzas. From the Roman necropolis that is the Alyscamps in Arles, France, to the Roman Forum itself. . .

ABOVE & RIGHT: Gucci Fall Winter 2015/2016 show, during Milan fashion week

ABOVE: Gucci runway show during the Milan Fashion Week Autumn/Winter 2015

From LA's Hollywood Boulevard, where as many celebrities walked the runway as sat in the front row, to Westminster Abbey in London. It was in summer 2016 that he curated the show in this most illustrious – and holy - of settings. This was the first time the Abbey had allowed its hallowed halls to show a fashion collection and was arguably Michele's finest hour. In the hushed cloisters of Westminster Abbey, Gucci cast a spell that signalled a new sort of craft. Where there was once Italian sexiness and chic, there were now grandma's reading glasses, neon tartans, flares, chintzy florals, cat sweaters and bows so large and camp and wide that they could have been straight out of a 1980s prom night. This was a never-seen-before Gucci. Still sexy, but in a slightly nerdy way, fringed with touches of Wes Anderson, British eccentricity, mystical spirituality and a certain, almost Jacobean sense of flirtatiousness. It certainly caught the imagination. After this show, the brand saw record sales.

Michele's aesthetic was making strides into unknown territories - pivoting to gender fluidity, bucolic imagery, and maximalism. It was just as well, as Gucci was in need of a fresh perspective for a new kind of customer - younger, less rigid, social-media savvy and eagerly looking for a sense of belonging to a new style tribe. Out went the slick, sleek, Americanised, highly-sexualised minimalism, and in its place came a romantic and gender-fluid, almost 'anything goes' vibe. This was perfectly encapsulated by Harry Styles photographed in a Gucci frock on the cover of Vogue. At the beginning of his tenure, Michele had been tasked with resurrecting the brand following a few seasons of underwhelming sales, attracting millennial customers while still maintaining Gucci's legacy as a premium brand. By 2017, all three aims had been achieved with the Business of Fashion reporting that Gucci *'aims to reach €10 billion in annual sales and replace LVMH's Louis Vuitton as the world's biggest luxury label.'*

Two thousand and eighteen saw Michele blazing another new trail on the runway. Featuring baby dragons, iguanas, third eyes, face masks and models carrying lifelike replicas of their own heads, the collection was a metaphor for how people construct their identities with the help of machines and other non-natural additions.

'We are the Dr Frankenstein of our own lives,' Michele said at the time.

Creating a waiting room-come-operating room area, Gucci described the show on Instagram.

'The concept reflects the work of a designer — the act of cutting, splicing and

RIGHT: Gucci Cruise 2017 fashion show at the Cloisters of Westminster Abbey on June 2, 2016 in London, England

reconstructing materials and fabrics to create a new personality and identity with them. The materials used are typical of an operating room and the environment around it: PVC on the walls and floors, fire doors with panic-bars, LED lamps, and plastic chairs like those in a waiting room.'

In 2019, Alessandro Michele revived Gucci's Beauty collection with a luscious 58-piece lipstick line-up. That same year saw the launch of the first Gucci fine jewellery collection, designed by Michele himself. Unlike the brand's attention-grabbing costume jewellery seen on the catwalk, this collection was elegant and restrained with the designer, in typical 'magpie' fashion, mixing-and-matching elements from his favourite eras.

'I was inspired by the idea that you were opening the safety deposit box of an old lady and it was full of beautiful things from different eras,' he explained.

Michele also had a flair for rule-breaking hook-ups. There was the fall 2021 Hacker Project with Balenciaga, and then a year later a collaboration with Adidas. Earlier in the pandemic, Michele enlisted the director Gus Van Sant to create a short film set in his hometown of Rome, indulging his love for movies. When he was taken to task for lifting from the Harlem couturier Dapper Dan, Gucci

RIGHT: Gucci runway during Milan fashion week Fall/Winter 2017/18

went into business with him. And it was during his tenure that the company launched the Vault, an online resale project for reworked treasures from the label's jet-set era heyday and an e-commerce emporium for on-the-rise designers that won his seal of approval.

Gucci celebrated its centenary in 2021. Kicking off its birthday celebrations, Gucci opened a new exhibit in the heart of Manhattan's Meatpacking District, tracking the Florentine house's most influential pieces over the decades. Between the Gucci-fied walls were velvet covered rooms, each curated with a distinct vibe. One was dedicated to the house's new fine jewellery offering, while another was reserved for its logo-emblazoned items, including the Balenciaga-hybrid Hacker Project pieces from the Fall 2021 collection.

'It isn't a revisionist attempt to rummage through the past: if anything, mine is a 'reverse' revisionism of the House's history, stitched back together by a piercing note, a melody, a refrain,' Michele revealed, explaining his inspiration for the Gucci 100 capsule collection. *'If I were to depict Gucci, for me it would be an eternal teenager who hangs out at places where music is heard and played.'*

Other centenary celebrations included pop-up shops in New York and London, 'Gucci Garden.

RIGHT: Part of the Balenciaga-hybrid Hacker project
OPP. PAGE: Gucci's Fake/Not collection, 2020

FAKE

ABOVE: Gucci show during the Milan fashion week Fall/Winter 2020/2021

ABOVE & RIGHT: Gucci Aria collection, 2021

Archetypes' - a multimedia experience in Florence reimagining 15 advertising campaigns from Michele's time as Creative Director of the brand, and a special fashion show in Beijing.

It was on Michele's watch that Ridley Scott's movie 'House of Gucci' was released and his influence was everywhere. It's star Lady Gaga wore his designs on the red carpet while friend and muse Jared Leto played Paolo Gucci. But in fashion, even the brightest stars don't shine forever. Perhaps because of Michele's agenda-setting success, Gucci's sales eventually started to dip, and in the wake of the pandemic, parent company Kering's shares fell as the brand slowed down. It's said that Michele was asked *'to initiate a strong design shift'*. However, this was not apparent during his last, highly emotional S/S 2023 show in late 2022. Featuring 68 sets of twins, it only doubled the impact of his continuing 'maximised' vision for the House.

In November 2022 Gucci announced that the brand and Michele were, after almost eight years, parting company. In the press release, Marco Bizzarri, then President and CEO of Gucci, thanked Michele for his dedication to the house over the past eight years, *'and for his vision, devotion, and unconditional love for this unique brand.'* François-Henri Pinault, chairman and CEO of Kering, which owns Gucci, stated that what Michele achieved would long be considered an important period in the history of the brand with *'his passion, his imagination, his ingenuity and his culture putting Gucci centre stage, where its place is. I wish him a great next chapter in his creative journey.'*

ABOVE: Promo poster for the film, House Of Gucci

Michele released his own statement.

'There are times when paths part ways because of the different perspectives each one of us may have. Today an extraordinary journey ends for me, lasting more than 20 years, within a company to which I have tirelessly dedicated all my love and creative passion. During this long period Gucci has been my home, my adopted family. To this extended family, to all the individuals who have looked after and supported it, I send my most sincere thanks, my biggest and most heartfelt embrace. Together with them I have wished, dreamed, imagined. Without them, none of what I have built would have been possible. To them goes my most sincere wish: may you continue to cultivate your dreams, the subtle and intangible matter that makes life worth living. May you continue to nourish yourselves with poetic and inclusive imagery, remaining faithful to your values. May you always live by your passions, propelled by the wind of freedom.'

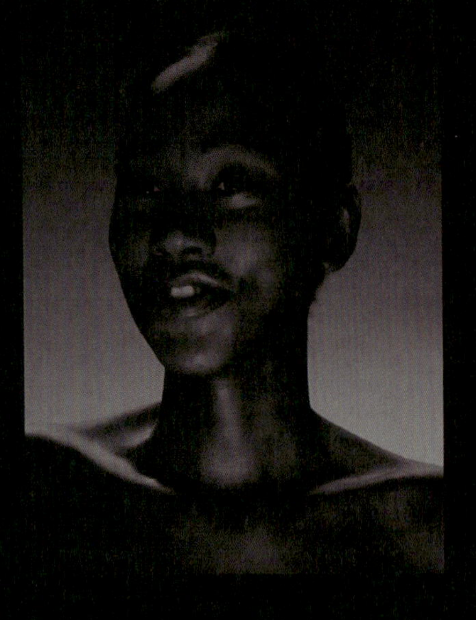

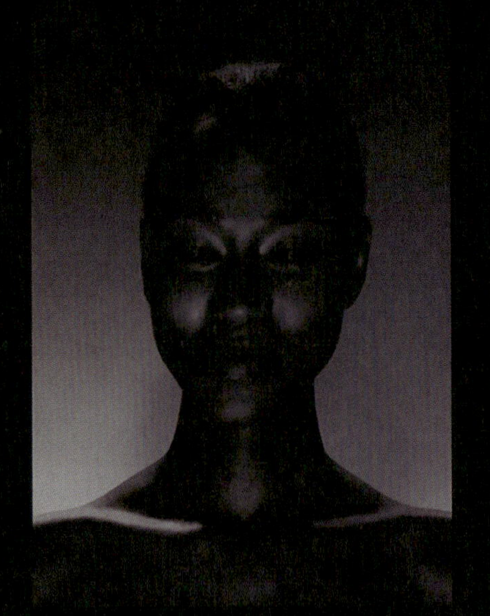

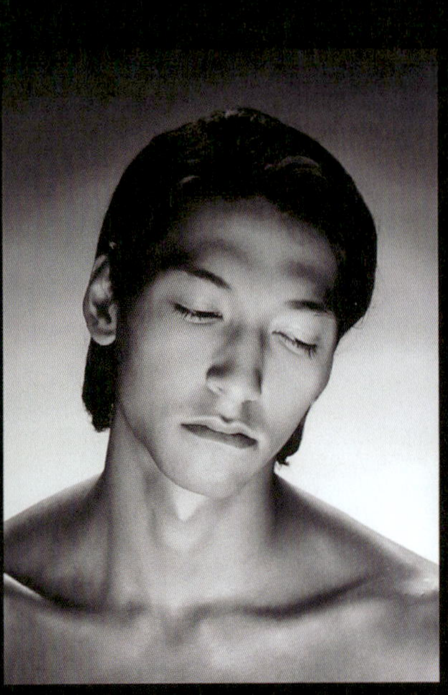

ABOVE: Alessandro Michele acknowledges the applause during the Gucci Twinsburg Show during Milan Fashion Week Spring/Summer 2023

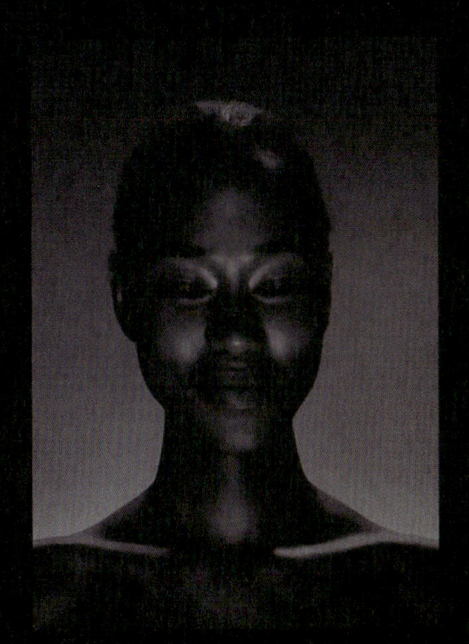
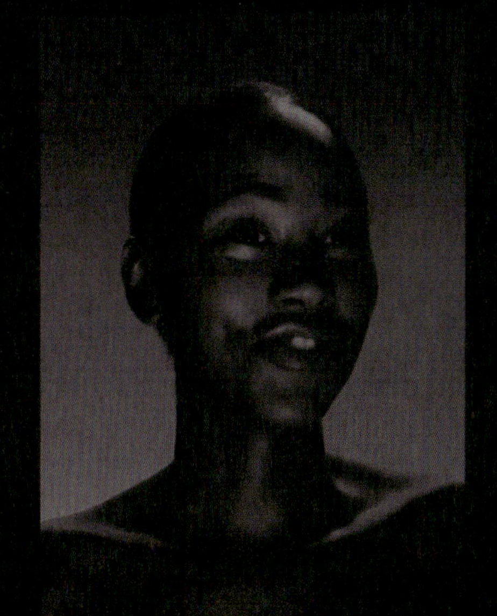
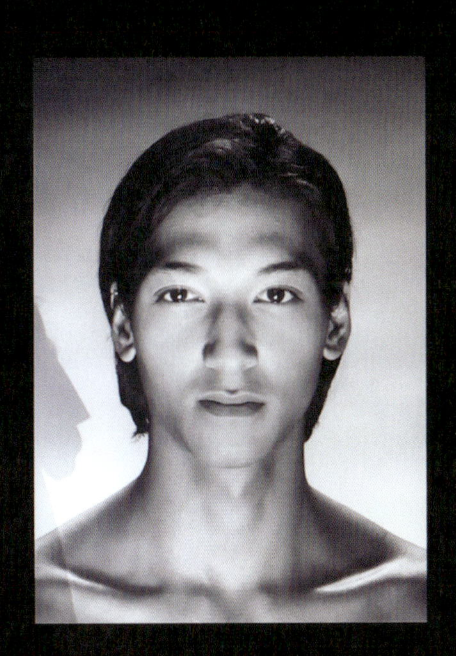
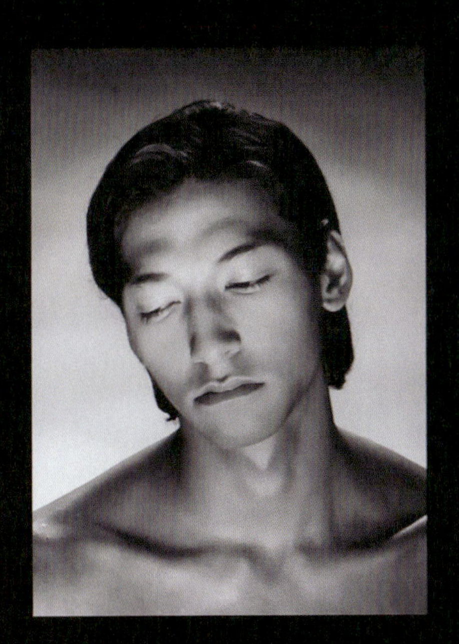

WHEN HARRY MET ALESSANDRO. . .

'Harry has an incredible sense of fashion'

Alessandro Michele on Harry Styles

The British Pop god and the Italian creative director became acquainted for the first time shortly after the release of the former's first solo album in 2017. It was, from the off, a genuine friendship rather than fleeting 'A' list liaison with the two immediately bonding over fashion as Styles pitched up for that first meet in a fake-fur coat which immediately wowed the designer. From then on, Alessandro and Harry were in constant Whatsapp contact and hung out together whenever their manically busy schedules allowed. Harry became a Gucci muse and went on to appear in a slew of campaigns, donning their designs both on the red carpet – his most memorable look being his flamboyant and frilly 2019 Met Gala outfit - and on tour. Perfectly encapsulating Michele's gender-fluid aesthetic, he famously appeared on the cover of Vogue in 2020 wearing a Gucci gown.

'Clothes are there to have fun with and experiment with and play with,' Styles explained. *'Any time you're putting barriers up in your own life, you're just limiting yourself. There's so much joy to be had in playing with clothes.'*

Words that could have come straight from Michele's mouth. No surprises then when it was announced that a Gucci/Styles collection was on the horizon. Launched in June 2022, it went on sale that November.

'The idea of working together came to me one day while we were talking on the phone,' Michele recalled. *'I proposed creating a "dream wardrobe" with him. We ended up with a mix of aesthetics, from 1970s pop and bohemia to the revision of the image of the gentleman in an overturned memory of men's tailoring. We were thinking for a long time of doing it, just for fun but it started to be something really concrete maybe a year before it was launched. It's a collection born from a creative relationship that self-generates from amusement and ends with the tangibility of a product.'*

Designer and popstar joined their initials to create the name of the collection - 'HA HA HA'. They also

enjoyed the comic element of the moniker which is, reportedly, how they often end their texts and messages to each other. It was, as Gucci put it, '*the written essence of the laughing face emoji.*'

The collection incorporated traditional English tailoring with dashes of romance and eccentricity. The double-breasted coats and jackets in Prince of Wales check and herringbone wools were juxtaposed with whimsical animal prints on shirts also boasting mother-of-pearl buttons, an appliquéd heart on a pair of boots, and a bold intarsia design on a sweater vest or tank top. Velvet suits in vibrant shades sat alongside printed pyjamas, bowling shirts, and pleated kilts. It was unmistakably Michele's Gucci with an umistakeable Styles-esque slant. Everywhere was the influence of swaggering '70s tailoring.

'I think it's just something natural, because we go crazy for jackets and beautiful pieces from that [1970s] world,' Michele said. *'Harry really represents everything we are saying. If you think about it, what did he do to be somewhat revolutionary and radically change his image? He put on a jacket.'*

He and Styles sent one another photos of 'eccentric men' from that era, with both, perhaps not entirely surprisingly, being fans of vintage.

'I love vintage shopping,' Michele revealed. *'I think that's really my place. You try to think about a home, your home, your place. Harry loves vintage, too. He has an incredible sense of fashion, he is obsessed with clothes. He keeps sketches and an archive, he could easily be a stylist or a designer and is very free, representative of this new generation that is interested in so many things. I have been observing his ability to combine items of clothing in a way that is out of the ordinary compared to the required standards of taste and common sense and the homogenisation of appearance.'*

Apart from 'liking' Michele's statement on leaving the House, Styles has not publicly commented on his friend's shock departure from Gucci.

LEFT: Harry Styles and Alessandro Michele at the 2019 Met Gala
ABOVE: Harry Styles featured in a Gucci advert

ABOVE: Harry Styles featured in a Gucci advert

A(NOTHER) NEW ERA

'Gucci and Kering are pleased to announce that Sabato de Sarno will assume the role of Creative Director for the House'

Statement released on the appointment of Gucci's new Creative Director, January 2023.

After a few months of fevered speculation, the identity of Gucci's latest Creative Director was announced in early 2023. Just as with Michele's appointment in 2015, Gucci looked behind-the-scenes for its next creative director, rather than choosing a household name or somebody who had already helmed another major fashion house – although unlike Giannini and Michele, Sabato de Sarno had not worked at Gucci in a lesser capacity before becoming Creative Director.

Personality-wise, he would seem to be more 'serious Giannini' than 'flamboyant Michele' or 'sexed-up' Ford. Born in Naples in 1983, he attended the IED European Institute of Design in Milan, where he studied fashion design, and graduated in 2005. Sabato's early exposure to the fashion industry provided him with the skills and knowledge needed to pursue a successful career. He joined Prada in 2005, later working for Dolce & Gabbana and, from 2009, he rose through the ranks at Valentino to become director of both men and women's ready-to-wear collections. At Valentino, he was known as Pierpaolo Piccioli's 'right-hand man' with sources saying he was also influential in bringing a more commercially contemporary aesthetic to Piccioli's work at Valentino. It is rumoured that de Sarno had major input into the 2022 Valentino wedding gown worn by Nicola Peltz at her marriage to Brooklyn Beckham.

A worthy apprenticeship, indeed, and one acknowledged by former Gucci CEO Marco Bizzarri. His statement announcing de Sarno's appointment revealed the brand's confidence in the designer's ability to successfully translate the heritage and legacy of Gucci.

'Having worked with a number of Italy's most renowned luxury fashion houses, he brings with him a vast and relevant experience,' it read. *'I am certain that through Sabato's deep understanding and appreciation for Gucci's unique legacy, he will lead our creative teams with a distinctive vision that will help write this*

RIGHT: Sabato de Sarno

RIGHT: Fall/Winter 2023/24, Milan fashion week

exciting next chapter, reinforcing the house's fashion authority while capitalising on its rich heritage.'

François-Henri Pinault, Chairman & CEO of Kering was equally enthusiastic – although he couldn't resist giving Gucci a big 'up' to begin with.

'One hundred and two years after Guccio Gucci opened his first store in Florence, Gucci remains one of the most iconic, prominent and influential luxury houses in the world,' read his statement. *'With Sabato de Sarno at the creative helm, we are confident that the House will continue both to influence fashion and culture through highly desirable products and collections, and to bring a singular and contemporary perspective to modern luxury.'*

According to an executive consultant at executive search company, it was in line with Kering's policy to hire an individual like de Sarno.

'We can assume that the arrival of Sabato De Sarno dovetails with Kering's strategy for Gucci' they said.

Responsible for 'defining and expressing the House's creative vision across the women's, men's, leather goods, accessories and lifestyle collections', de Sarno's response, publicly at least, seemed almost humble.

ABOVE & RIGHT: Gucci Womenswear Spring/Summer 2024, during Milan fashion week

'I am deeply honoured to take on the role as creative director of Gucci,' he said in a statement. *'I am proud to join a house with such an extraordinary history and heritage, that over the years has been able to welcome and cherish values I believe in. I am touched and excited to contribute my creative vision for the brand.'*

The first hint at the look and feel of De Sarno's Gucci came in the timing of the announcement. Sabato means Saturday in Italian, and Kering released the news outside the working week, on a Saturday morning. It was the kind of quirky move that Michele, who always worked to his own rhythm, may well have teased. A hint, perhaps, from de Sarno that he, too, intends to do things very much his own way and add a deeply personal touch to his collections.

While de Sarno got to grips with his new position and concentrated on what would be his first collection for the House, due to be launched in September 2023, eight months earlier, in February 2023, Gucci had unveiled its first women's ready-to-wear collection since the departure of Alessandro Michele. This collection, created by the fashion house's design team, was regarded as a bridge, linking Michele and de Sarno. The result? A kind of reworking of Gucci's Greatest Hits, combining the rich heritage of the

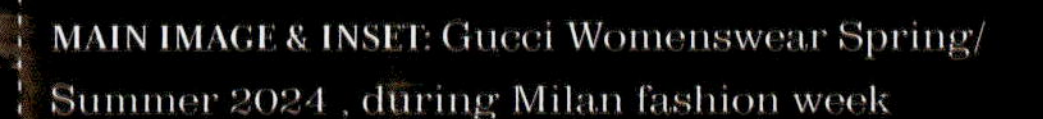

MAIN IMAGE & INSET: Gucci Womenswear Spring/Summer 2024 , during Milan fashion week

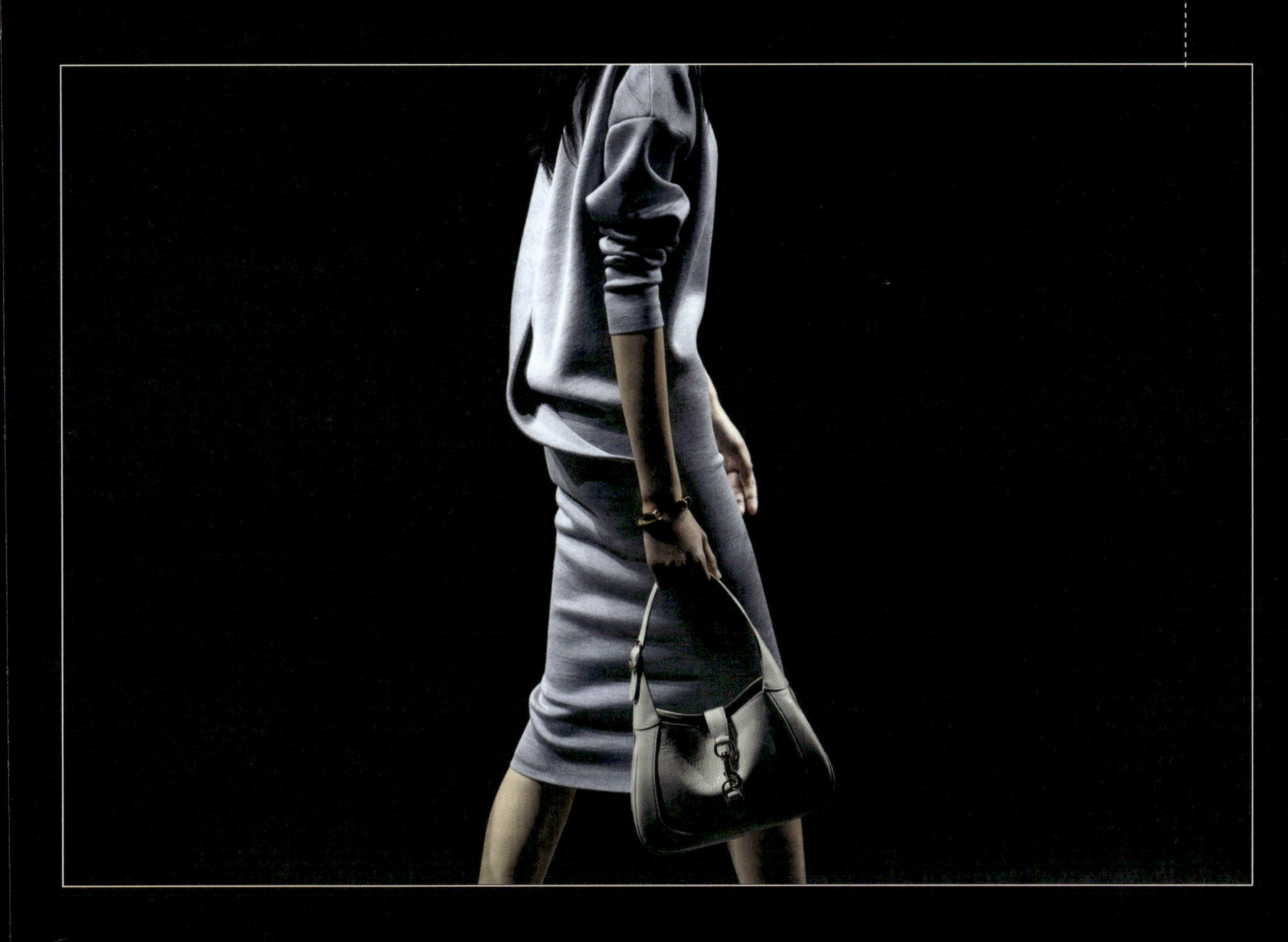

ABOVE & RIGHT: Gucci collection show during Milan fashion week, Menswear Autumn/Winter 2024/2025

brand during its 'Dolce Vita' period with a feel of Ford sexiness and some Michele eccentricity added to the mix.

Historical cues from past Gucci collections were recalled throughout the range, interpreted and observed through a contemporary gaze. The first look to hit the stage arrived uncovered, sporting a barely-there bra-top emblazoned with Gucci's interlocking emblem, silk maxi skirt with sexy slit, and leather gloves finished with metallic fingertips. An apt homage to Tom Ford. As were the sheer, flesh-revealing dresses, tight-fitting jersey tops and slim-fitting pencil skirts. Michele's quirksome influences could be seen in oversized faux fur coats dyed neon blue, black and yellow, startling lavender and discoloured purple. Bustled hips were also pure Michele as was the mammoth shoulder padding, crystalized adornments were seen in the form of dramatic choker necklaces, draped frayed brooches – some of which were even crafted into an entire fringe overcoat. Perhaps the most Michele-esque pieces, however, were the massive feathered millinery confections in black and blush pink. While the collection was certainly a mixture between both Ford and Michele's visions of the brand, Ford-era inspiration was the most present - most explicitly seen in the re-issuing of the Gucci horsebit clutch bag from his era as creative director.

Going forward, Gucci seems focused on the sexuality that has dominated this period in its history. Therefore, it would seem that a new era of sensuality is on its way - with a Sabato spin in order for Gucci to elevate the brand and perhaps shift to a more classic and formal silhouette to reflect the zeitgeist. But like those who have gone before him, de Sarno will chose to incorporate into his vision his versions of those classic La Casa Gucci icons– the Jackie bag, the Bamboo, the Stripe, the double G logo, the Horsebit, and the Flora. . .

ABOVE & RIGHT: Gucci collection show during Milan fashion week, Menswear Autumn/Winter 2024/2025

ABOVE: Gucci collection show during Milan fashion week, Menswear Autumn/Winter 2024/2025

GUCCI BY NUMBERS

538

The number of Gucci stores across the world

117

The number of Gucci stores in the USA

26

The number of Gucci stores in the UK

36

In December 2019, Gucci sued three dozen websites selling fake Gucci products

3,134

The cost in US dollars of Gucci's 'Genius Jeans' when launched in 1998. This earned the legwear an entry in the Guinness Book of Records, setting a record as the most expensive pair of jeans to ever go on sale. The jeans were distressed, ripped, and covered with African-inspired beads

Figures correct at time of going to press

4

Gucci is the fourth most valuable high fashion brand in the world. Louis Vuitton is first, followed by Hermès, Chanel and then Gucci.

177.8

The height, in millimetres, of Gucci's Fall 2016 wedges

103

The age of La Casa Gucci

17.8 BILLION

The value of the brand in US dollars in 2022

118

The number of Gucci perfumes and colognes in their fragrance base. The earliest edition 'Gucci No 1 for Women' was created in 1974 while the most recent 'Where My Heart Beats', using 100% carbon-captured alcohol, went on sale In April 2023.

55

The percentage of leather goods that make up the Maison's overall output

17,953

Approximately the amount of Gucci employees world-wide

1

The number of Michelin stars at the Gucci Osteria in Florence

75 MILLION

The budget in US dollars for the 2021 film 'House of Gucci'

THE MAGNIFICENT SEVEN

The seven, truly iconic Gucci handbags. . .

The Bamboo 1947

The House continues to forge creative expressions of the Gucci Bamboo 1947. Handcrafted since its inception, the signature top handle bag still embodies the same experimental spirit and artisanal excellence today. Alessandro Michele unveiled the new Gucci Bamboo 1947 in February 2022, reimagined in his signature paintbox palette, in various sizes and with the addition of a long strap.

Gucci 1955 Horsebit

The 1955 Horsebit, one of the more recent launches from the house, is based on archival designs from 1955. It has a simple saddle-shaped silhouette, with an elegant flap and equestrian-inspired horsebit hardware. Thanks to its classic design, this is an It bag that has longevity. It comes in simple leather versions, printed versions with leather trims and different sizes.

Gucci Jackie

The Jackie is another archival piece from the '60s. It was initially named after former FLOTUS Jackie Kennedy and has been an iconic Gucci item for decades. Back in 2020, it was relaunched with a bit of a makeover—Michele introducing pastel leather options, as well as the classics, and cleaner lines with an additional strap and that stylishly elegant gold clasp. Years on and it's still one of the brand's bestsellers. Harry Styles has one in black.

Gucci Dionysus

The Dionysus is a Michele original which, although a modern classic, has an eccentric vintage feel due, in part, to its structured design. The shoulder bag has a flap fixed with a tiger-head clasp which is an homage to the Greek god Dionysus, who crossed the river Tigris on a tiger.

Gucci Marmont

Centred around the brand's archival GG symbol, the Gucci Marmont line includes totes, shoulder bags, bucket bags, circular shapes and mini designs. Some of the line's most popular models come in classic cream and black leathers.

Gucci Ophidia

Ophidia debuted in 2018 and combines two defining Gucci motifs - the GG supreme canvas and Web stripe - making the bag instantly recognisable. Boasting a shiny gold GG Marmont tab, this is a great option for those who like the brand's more retro-inspired pieces with its square shape being very vintage Gucci.

Gucci Diana

The Gucci Diana, named after the late Princess and first presented by the House in 1991, features the distinctive bamboo handle of the first Gucci purse, married with a tote. Combining various Gucci emblems, the bag was reimagined by Alessandro Michele in three different sizes with removable, neon leather belts, which is a nod to the functional bands that once came with the original bag to maintain the shape of the handles.